To Josh
Cars have always
been fun.
Murv Perry

Murv's Motoring Memories

Murvin H. Perry

JOHNSON CITY, TENNESSEE

ISBN 0-932807-72-0

Printed in the United States of America

1 2 3 4 5 6 7 8 9 0

To my parents, Earl H. and Lorraine Eichel Perry

ACKNOWLEDGMENTS

I am indebted to my editor, JoLinda Cheryl Lewis (Sherry), for assistance in preparing this manuscript for publication, to my son Scott for scanning the manuscript into a computer file for typesetting, to my friend Jim Webber who allowed me to use his computer to edit the copy, to my wife, Rita, who read and critiqued the stories as they were written, to members of the East Tennessee Regional Group of the Early Ford V8 Club of America whose appreciation of ''Motor Memories'' prompted me to continue developing the stories, and to David L. Lewis, editor of ''Ford Country'' for **Cars and Parts,** and George H. Dammann of Crestline Publishers for words of encouragement when I proposed these stories for a book.

CONTENTS

PREFACE

Among the tales passed along in our family are stories of the car, obviously descended from a horse-drawn buggy, that came with a whip socket on the dash — and of the neighbor with a violent temper who took a sledgehammer to his Model T when it wouldn't start. Still unenlightened, he used an axe to drive the spark plugs into the block of a balky pump engine.

Those little snatches of irrationality helped parents and grandparents feel better about their own efforts to cope with a bewildering world of promise and problems which the automobile posed.

The stories in this collection are true. I have recounted them as accurately as aging memory will permit. I share them, just for fun, with those who have discovered the automobile to be a demanding, but enjoyable, mistress.

MODEL T MEMORIES

STEERING WHEEL

When I was five or six years old, I used to play in the car, pretending I was driving. With great enthusiasm, I rocked the steering wheel rapidly from side to side, much to the consternation of my father, who felt such treatment would increase the "play" in the steering.

The Model T we owned at the time was of uncertain history. It had a special lock on the steering wheel. The top of the planetary gear case under the steering wheel, which provided a reduction in the steering ratio, had been replaced with a bulging cast aluminum cover with a tumbler lock protruding to the right side. The key had not come with the car, and since the wheel appeared to be in unlocked position, the whole thing was ignored.

One day, while playing at driving, I pulled back sharply on the wheel. To my dismay, it came out by the roots. The little stub shaft with the small gear on the end was still attached to the wheel. I was panicked because I thought I had broken the car. Carefully, I put it back in place. It seemed to go in all right and it still seemed to turn as before. I quietly slipped out of the car and was careful not to mention the incident to anyone.

Sometime later, as we were chugging down a country road between a barbed wire fence and a cornfield, I remembered the wheel and said, "Daddy, if you pull back on the steering wheel, it comes right out."

"Awww, it does not," my father replied as he pulled up on the wheel and sat holding it in bewilderment as the car ran off the road and became entangled in the fence.

For years I puzzled over the fact that the stub shaft which came out with the wheel lacked the flange that held it in the case. In its place there was a recess about one-fourth inch wide and of similar depth. Many years, and many Model T experiences later, I concluded that the design of the device was such that in "unlocked" position, the lock engaged that recess and held the wheel in place, whereas in the "locked" position, the shaft was freed so the driver could take the steering wheel with him when he parked the car. This insured that his vehicle could not be driven off by anyone else.

MY FIRST DRIVE

I was about seven years old when I got my first opportunity to drive the Model T. One of Dad's few indulgences was hunting pheasants in the fields and farm country of rural South Dakota.

In the prosperous days of steady employment, he had paid a staggering $50 for a new 1910 Remington 12-gauge pump shotgun. In the tightest years of the depression, he would justify spending a dollar for a box of 25 shells by counting all the meals we could anticipate from the game he bagged. Mother would jaw at him for wasting money if he missed three or four times.

Occasionally the hunting was conducted in large groups including Grandpa and Grandma Eichel, Mother and Dad, his brother Bruce, brother-in-law Ed Schulz, two of Mother's younger unmarried sisters and sometimes their beaux. Only the menfolks carried guns. We younger ones, along with the women, walked between them as "flushers" as they strung out in a line and walked through the corn rows or grain fields that provided cover for the pheasants.

Since Grandpa Eichel had lost part of one foot in a railroad accident, he found walking the fields too much for him, so he and Grandma and Mother assumed the task of moving the cars along the country roads to meet the hunters as they moved through the fields.

Grandpa carried a 16-gauge single-shot Iver Johnson shotgun. He would arrive at the end of the field before the hunters and station himself so that game that ran ahead of the hunters would be flushed, and he could quickly bag his limit.

At other times, Dad hunted alone. Mother and the kids, baby Dale, brother Lyle, and I would accompany him to the country in the Model T. He would drive the back roads until he found a likely place for pheasants, such as a thicket with open fields around it. He would walk through the thicket and flush the birds into the fields at the edge.

If the thicket stretched a long way, Mother would follow the road with the car and meet him at the other end.

One day he flushed a large number of birds from a small cluster of plum trees and followed them across a long grassy area as they flew

Preparing to hunt pheasants — Jerry Nichols and Andy Dahlbol pose with shotguns on the Shoemaker farm north of Bruce, S.D., about 1921.

to a weed patch about a half mile away. He had left the Ford idling. Since Mother was occupied with my brothers, I slipped under the wheel and pushed down on the low pedal carefully, to start the car moving down the road after him.

I had to stand and hang onto the wheel in order to reach the pedal, but as the car began to inch forward, I stepped down bravely, pulled down the gas (the throttle lever just below the steering wheel) and steered along the rutted country road. Mother gasped when the car began to move, but she allowed me to continue, which I did for the few minutes it took to catch up with Dad, who by then was waiting a half mile down the road. It may have been only a half mile, but what did that matter? I had driven a car! Life would never be the same.

DAD'S FIRST CAR

Dad's first car, the one in which he courted Mother and the one he drove for the next five years, was a 1920 Model T roadster. He bought it brand new from the Ford dealership in Arlington, S.D., for $365, cash he had saved from day wages on farms in the community.

Since Dad was only 20 years old and had never driven a car, when he took delivery of his purchase, the dealer rode with him for a short drive to check him out.

All went well around the block until they approached the garage door. Dad applied the brakes, but nothing happened. The car coasted right on by.

Dad's first car — Earl and Lorraine Perry with the 1920 Model T roadster about 1921 on the farm near Bruce, S.D.

"Don't worry," the dealer said. "Go around again, and next time you'll get the hang of it."

The second try was no better than the first. There seemed to be a slight braking effect as Dad pressed the pedal, but the car continued to coast past the garage door.

On the third trip around the block, the dealer suggested that maybe the brake band needed adjustment, and that for an emergency stop, Dad could use the reverse pedal. As they approached the garage for the third time, he pressed the reverse pedal.

The effect was the same. There was a slight slowing of the vehicle, and then it went into a freewheeling coast that ceased only when the car had finally lost momentum.

Trying to back up to the overshot door was similarly ineffective. The motor spun, the transmission groaned, but the car did not move in reverse. Carefully they inched the car back, into the garage for a checkup. Examination revealed that the key had not been installed in the spline in the left rear axle.

When the axle turned forward, the nut tightened sufficiently to hold the wheel fixed on the tapered axle. When the torque was reversed by the braking action or by reverse gear, the nut loosened and the wheel spun on the axle.

Since both the brake and reverse acted on the drive shaft, the differential passed the torque to the free axle and left the one that was anchored to the wheel unaffected.

T-TREK IN SEARCH OF EMPLOYMENT

Some photographs from our family album show two Model Ts with boxes or platforms where the back seat should be, loaded with beds, stoves, and other household gear a la John Steinbeck and **Grapes of Wrath** in the 1930s. However, it wasn't 1930; it was 1924, and despite the desperate circumstances suggested by the prototype pictures from **Grapes of Wrath,** equipment on this trip included a camera and funds for film.

Although I was only two at the time, I have three distinct recollections of the summer. Grandpa Eichel had quit farming and taken a brief fling at running a restaurant in a small South Dakota town. The restaurant prospered while a road crew was building a highway in the area, but it went downhill when the road was finished. Both Grandpa and Dad, who had worked for the road contractor, found themselves without many

Ready for the road — The Perry family heads west to find work in the spring of 1924.

The family makes camp along the way — The camp served as headquarters while the menfolk sought work in the area.

prospects in Aurora, S.D., when the highway project was completed and the contractor folded his operations.

With the prospect of employment ''out west,'' they packed their women and children and what belongings they would need into boxes on the back of the old Fords and set off in search of their fortunes.

(Mother's two younger sisters and Grandma and Grandpa made up one foursome, with Dad and Mother, myself, and the youngest of my six brothers making up the other.) What couldn't be carried was left with family or friends remaining behind.

I do not remember the setting of camps along the way or the tornado that blew away the tent, leaving my mother huddled with two small boys in the lee of the iron cook stove (the only thing not carried away by the storm). But I have a clear memory of arriving at the landing at Ft. Pierre, S.D., where a ferryboat carried cars across the Missouri River. There was considerable discussion among the adults as to whether or not we should board the ferry and go on west or turn back to some of the towns we had just passed through. I remember a tall black touring car with its back curtain wobbling back and forth as it bounced over the ruts of the landing and drove aboard the ferry. I was disappointed when the gate to the boat was closed and we watched it paddle away.

The venture turned out successfully. Dad found work with a farmer in Highmore, and we continued to live in the tent for the rest of the summer, despite the tornado. Local folks called it a ''cyclone'' in those days.

All the comforts of home — Camping equipment included mattresses and a kerosene heater.

Across the wide Missouri — Ferry boat plies the Missouri River at Ft. Pierre, S.D., in 1924.

Home again — The Perrys arrive back in Bruce in the fall of 1924, after the summer in the fields of Central South Dakota.

Grandpa got a job tending the light plant at Miller, S.D., and Grandma was hired as a cook in a local restaurant. They had an apartment on the upper floor of the restaurant building.

Grandpa's job provided one other memory. I was fascinated by the great spinning flywheels on the generators and the little flyball governors on the engines in the noisy powerhouse. I could see the stack on top of the plant from Grandma's apartment. I thought that big long pipe sticking up must be the source of the whistle which was sounded by the plant each morning, noon, and evening.

Another memory involves the trip back "home," when the farm work had run out. The exact date is hazy, but it was probably early fall. We were dressed in warm clothing; I remember a particular stocking cap and sweater. The Ford was completely open, because its top had been blown away in the cyclone and was never replaced. The trip of about 150 miles took all day, and when we arrived at Grandma Perry's place in Bruce, I was very uncomfortable because my leg had gone to sleep.

CRANKING WOUNDS

A Model-T-inflicted broken arm was quite common in the days of my youth, but only once did I see a T unwind with a vicious, backward crank-revolving kick. That was when I neglected to "put the spark up" (move the spark lever all the way up to fully retard the spark).

Although I escaped that particular injury during the many years I cranked an old Ford, I was twice wounded in another way while starting a cranky Model T.

One of the secrets for starting an obstinate T was to jack up one of the back wheels and throw the hand brake lever all the way forward. This was particularly helpful if you were starting the engine on the "mag." It released the rearward force on the clutch throwout bearing and allowed the flywheel magnets to run closer to the coils of the magneto, increasing the current for ignition. The amount of current increase depended upon the amount of end play in the crankshaft bearings.

A second advantage was that the wheel provided additional flywheel momentum if you were spinning the crank. Even if you were starting on battery ignition, the added flywheel effect often made the difference between an easy start and a lot of cranking.

To facilitate jacking the car for starting, my grandfather made a lever jack from some six-foot two-by-fours which made it possible to lift the wheel with one giant motion of the lever. The only problem with this arrangement was that it took two people to get the car down off the jack after the engine was started. One had to sit in the driver's seat and depress the low pedal far enough to release the clutch, and then apply the brake to stop the spinning wheel. The other then released the jack and lowered the wheel. Technically it should have been possible to stop the wheel by pulling the hand brake lever all the way back, as there was a cam device that was supposed to release the clutch as the rear wheel brakes were applied. However, I never did see one that was properly adjusted.

When I was about 12 years old, I thought I could handle the lowering chore. I did, but was barely heavy enough to hold down the lever so that I could withdraw the pin that held the jack in the elevated position. I developed a technique of bouncing on it, quickly pulling the pin, and riding the lever up as the car dropped to the ground. One day I misjudged the bounce, and the rebounding lever hit me on the side of the head. I saw stars the astronomers haven't discovered yet.

Made cautious by this experience, I successfully handled the jacking and starting chores for several years until, in fact, the jack aged to the point where the wood mechanism that secured it in the up position deteriorated. Instead of repairing it, I jury-rigged it with a piece of bailing wire. Unfortunately, the wire wasn't up to the task and let go one morning just as I was preparing to lower the wheel. It caught me under the chin that time!

When I volunteered for the Navy in World War II, I was rejected until the dentist could make some temporary repairs for my missing teeth.

A FORD GOES TO COLLEGE

A 1912 Model T Ford is the prized possession of the student association at South Dakota State University at Brookings, and although school officials have recently spent more than $1,250 refurbishing that ancient automobile, it continues to be displayed in a manner that car aficionados would consider sacrilegious.

With great glory, but little dignity, the Ford assumes a central role in the celebration of "Hobo Day," the annual college homecoming. Dressed in the most outlandish rags they can improvise, the students at this agricultural college each fall stage one of the most colorful spectacles of the Northwest. The old T, affectionately christened "the Bummobile," serves as regal transportation for the king and queen of homecoming. Each year it conveys its cargo of ragged royalty through a three-mile parade in the morning and to the stadium for the football game and coronation ceremonies at half-time.

The T is equipped as it came from the factory, with acetylene headlights and polished brass radiator and windshield braces. The only

Limousine service — President Dwight Eisenhower is shown at the wheel of the "Bummobile" during a visit to the Brookings, S.D., campus in 1950.

Still going — The "Bummobile" is made ready for another homecoming.

modifications have been to move the coil box under the hood and to install a battery and switch to allow running on either battery or magneto.

Its most recent refurbishing was financed by a gift from some graduates, who raised the money by selling souvenir photographs of couples posed in the old Ford during the Fabulous Fifties Reunion in the summer of 1987.

The car was presented to the student association in 1939 by Frank Weigel of Flandreau, S.D., a farmer who had admired the Hobo Day celebration. It required a major overhaul and repainting in 1949 after an incident that nearly ended the saga of the famous old Ford.

On Thursday morning, October 28, 1948, members of the student body at State discovered that the garage that held the Bummobile had been raided by fraternity men from the rival University of South Dakota at Vermillion. The venerable vehicle had been stolen. A week of frantic bargaining followed, during which the president of State appealed to the student body of the University to make a sportsmanlike offer for ransom and return of the car.

Newspapers seized the story and the columns were filled with statements from University supporters to the effect that they would paint the car bright red (their school's color), drive it in their own homecoming parade, then dismantle it and present each University student with a nut, bolt, or bearing as a souvenir of their complete humiliation of State.

Search parties from State combed the University town for the hiding place of the prize. The National Guard was alerted to quell violence in case State students attempted a reprisal raid. (There was good reason. The previous fall, Sioux Falls police had returned to headquarters in cruisers painted yellow and blue when they tried to halt a raiding party from State which was painting a dormitory at Augustana College in State's blue and gold colors.)

At last a settlement was reached which allowed University students to drive the car in their homecoming parade. State students cast and presented a trophy attesting to the car coup and, in exchange for the Ford's safe return, further agreed to return the crest of a fraternity house (which they had "captured" the year before).

The rough usage experienced in the theft necessitated a complete overhaul and repainting for the Bummobile. Its front wheels had been lashed to the rear bumper of a modern car, and it had been towed the 90 miles from Brookings to Vermillion at many times the speed at which it was designed to travel. New parts were not available, so the old connecting rods were re-babbitted, and the body was sanded and painted a new shiny black.

During summer months, the Model T is filled with beard-growing members of the State band and sent to fairs and local celebrations as an animated advertisement for the State homecoming.

Visitors to the campus during preparations for the celebration, including governors and presidents, are apt to be met at the airport by six bearded students in the Bummobile and treated to a ride in the ancient Ford. President Dwight Eisenhower, on a visit to the campus in the early 1950s, took the wheel himself and followed directions to the campus as he drove the old T through the streets of Brookings.

OLD STUBS

CYCLONE

Stubs was part some kind of bulldog, bull terrier, or possibly pit bull, and part who knows what. He joined the family as a pup when I was only a year old. He had short black hair with a white collar and chest, and there was a hint of tan at his jowls. His name came from his three-inch tail (which was all that was left after he had been ''docked'' as such dogs were customarily groomed in those days). He grew to about 40 pounds.

I don't remember his early days, but pictures from the family album show me romping with him.

When Dad's road construction job ran out, he loaded his family into the old Ford and trekked west to find work. Stubs went along with us. We traveled in the 1920 T roadster Dad had bought nearly five years earlier. The tonneau had been replaced with a box made of wood, in which tents, beds, a stove, and other necessary gear was carried. A board fastened from fender to fender along the left running board provided an additional compartment for small things necessary for life on the road.

When we broke camp one morning, somewhere west of Miller, S.D., Stubs was not to be found. With some reluctance, Mother and Dad moved on without him, deciding that he was probably too much trouble anyway. Two days later and more than 20 miles down the road, we were awakened early in the morning by a dog's bark. To our surprise we saw Stubs coming up the railroad track, baying in delight at finding us.

At Highmore, Dad found work with a farmer, and we camped in a school yard near the fields where he was employed. Days passed in pleasurable succession until the cyclone hit. (''Cyclone'' was the term used in the Midwest during the early '20s to describe the twisters that plague the plains on hot summer days.)

Our camp was arranged around a small cast-iron stove of the kind

Me and Stubs — Stubs as a one-year-old pup and the author at age two.

known as a "laundry stove," because its two-lidded top was just the right size to hold a wash boiler of water. It was low, so lifting was minimized. It suited our camping purposes.

A wall tent about 10 by 14 feet sheltered a bed, a folding army cot on which my brother and I slept, a crude table, and a couple of stools.

Although the bright July day gave no hint of an impending storm, Mother noted that Stubs was restless. He whined as she placed me on the cot for a nap. To her annoyance, he climbed on the cot with me and snarled when she ordered him off. He crouched beside the cot and watched me as clouds began to gather and to threaten.

Just as the storm struck, he jumped up and dragged me from the cot and crouched over me next to the stove. In the tornado's first blast, the tent pegs gave way and the canvas ripped and followed the wind. The heavy ridge pole of the tent crashed down, smashing the cot on which I had been sleeping.

In the fields three or four miles away, Dad and his boss clung to the machines and tried to calm the frantic horses. When the storm passed, he cranked the battered car (its top had been torn off by the wind) and raced to the campsite, filled with apprehension as to what he would find.

After the storm — the author in borrowed clothes on the prairie near Highmore, S.D., after a tornado swept away the family's camp in the summer of 1924.

The stove was all that remained. The tent, the beds, clothing, and utensils were scattered for miles. Some things were never found. Mother was crouched in the lee of the stove, with one infant son on each arm. She was being comforted by the pup who had refused to be abandoned.

I don't know what powers of intuition or premonition Stubs possessed, but it was certain he had saved me from serious injury or perhaps worse. He had earned his place in the family for the rest of his 14-year life.

KING OF THE ROAD

In 1925, Dad got a job maintaining a section of the gravel roads newly graded by the county. A county truck unhitched a new grader just inside our gate. It was a fascinating machine, with two large hand wheels to raise and lower the blade, levers to adjust the angle of the blade to cut down the roadbed or smooth loose material across it, and a pivot to swing the blade from one side to the other.

It was to be drawn by four horses, one team ahead of the other. For the next five years Dad plied the roads radiating to the north and west, stretching from our village to the county borders, and east to the KT (short for ''King of Trails,'' the major north-south highway, now U.S. 77). In all, he regularly ''graded'' about 30 miles of two-lane gravel road.

Stubs assumed it was his responsibility to patrol the roads with Dad. He accompanied the grader every day, ranging along the roadside to chase gophers, rabbits, and an occasional fox, sniffing out caches of moonshine local bootleggers had stashed in culverts and other pick-up places. He regularly whipped all farm dogs along the way; big or small, their size made no difference to him. His bull terrier instincts gave him a fighting skill that enabled him to intimidate even the largest St. Bernard or German police dog. It was this fighting instinct and his domination of all roadside dogs that eventually did him in.

In 1930, Grandpa Eichel was hired to manage the county poor farm.

Visiting Grandpa and Grandma — The Perry family is shown with Stubs and the family car on a visit to grandparents, Henry and Ida Eichel at the Brookings County farm near Aurora, S.D., in 1932. From left, (back row) Earl, baby Wayne, Lorraine, (front row) Lyle, Dale, Murvin.

He found the buildings overrun by rats. To eliminate them, he borrowed Stubs, who took to the chore with delight. Grandpa would go into one of the outbuildings late at night, switch on the lights, and encourage Stubs to catch the rats as they scurried into hiding. He was credited with 16 in one three- or four-minute foray.

I don't know how long Stubs stayed on at the farm after the rats had been eliminated, but the six of us—I now had three brothers—visited regularly in the 1925 Model T touring car that had replaced the roadster in 1926.

Occasionally he would try to follow the car when we left for home, but he was always sternly ordered to go back. Once, we spotted him loping through the fields about 30 yards off, on a course parallel to the road, nearly five miles along the way home. I don't think he forgave us for hauling him back and tying him up so he couldn't follow again.

When the horse grader was replaced by motor-driven units that could cover more ground, Dad took up farming and Stubs took on new chores. He accompanied me and my brothers as we herded the milk cows to graze along the railroad tracks when the pasture was short. He turned an aggressive young Holstein when she regularly broke for the nearby cornfields, and he nipped the heels of a pokey Guernsey when she lagged behind the herd. When the cattle were penned, he resolutely chased foolish leghorn hens from Mother's garden, with great flapping and squawking.

More years passed. One fall day, when Dad and a crew of the neighbors were threshing, Stubs, as usual, accompanied the bundle wagons to the oats field. At lunchtime the crew unhitched their teams and tied them to the bundle racks to feed while they loaded into the old Model T and drove the mile or two to the house for lunch. Despite his advancing age, Stubs ran beside the car.

As they passed a neighboring farmyard, a dog ran out to challenge Stubs. They tangled in a flurry of barks, bites, and yelps in the center of the road directly in front of the lunch-bound crew's car. The driver tried to stop, but there wasn't time. Both dogs were killed.

We consoled ourselves that a 14-year-old dog couldn't have had too much time left, and that if Stubs had had a choice, he would have elected to end it all in a good fight.

A GOOD EXAMPLE

There is another story about old Stubs that deserves telling. When I was young, I observed with some smugness that my father did not frequent the local pool hall as did most of the fathers of my contemporaries, wasting time in an unsavory environment in unproductive pursuits like snooker and bawdy conversation.

There was a reason. When we first moved into town for the winter (summer was spent in the road construction camps), Dad did join the local menfolks in the town pool hall. He was accompanied by faithful Stubs, by then three or four years old with a settled demeanor, no longer a clumsy, curious pup.

Despite his obedient and serene disposition, the pool hall was a boring place for Stubs. It was warm and comfortable, but there was no provision for some things dogs just have to do. In the crowded, smoky atmosphere of the place, it was difficult to get his master's attention when he wished to exit the place and do his business.

There was, however, what to Stubs seemed like a suitable alternative. In front of the counter on which the cash register rested, the proprietor had placed a pressed-paper container of hard candy. It was about a foot in diameter and almost two feet tall.

One evening Stubs decided the candy pail would do in a pinch. He lifted his hind leg and ruined a whole bucket of candy. Many of the patrons were highly amused, because the proprietor was a known pinch-penny who was obviously pained by the impossibility of salvaging the candy. Despite the fact that Dad offered to pay for the loss, he barred Stubs from the establishment.

Dad's attitude was that if his dog wasn't welcome, he wasn't either, and he never went back into the place. Perhaps the motive was not quite so worthy as we assumed when we were young, but all seven of his sons emulated their father and avoided hanging out in the pool hall. We always credited Dad for the good example. Perhaps we should have thanked Stubs.

I REMEMBER GRANDPA EICHEL

THE KING CAB

The King Cab with room for extra passengers has made the Japanese mini-pickup truck a serviceable family vehicle. Grandpa Eichel had a similar idea in 1925, although he laid it out differently.

He bought a brand new Model T chassis, and since he was a reasonably skilled carpenter, he planned to construct the body himself.

I recall the day he and Grandma drove it into the yard; it looked absolutely naked. The steering wheel stuck up in front of the dash, and there was nothing behind the firewall. Grandpa and Grandma sat on a wood box that just fit over the gas tank. (I have the distinct impression, although I can't prove it at this date, that it was the crate in which a new cream separator from Montgomery Ward had been shipped.)

Grandpa had purchased the truck in Watertown, about 50 miles from Bruce where we lived at the time. I don't have any details of what must have been a two-hour open air drive on that running gear, but Grandma was bubbling with excitement. She had done some shopping in the big city, and she brought along little gifts for her two grandsons. Grandpa was full of plans for the truck he was going to build.

The bed of the truck was quite traditional. It was built as farm wagon boxes in the region were built, of four-inch tongue-and-grooved fir flooring boards with iron reinforcements. I suspect the iron parts had been salvaged from a farm wagon that had become unserviceable.

Since there were still two unmarried daughters, the family automobile had to be a four-passenger vehicle. Grandpa solved this by making the cab, also built of fir flooring boards, nearly as wide as the bed (almost seven feet). It would seat four people side by side. One sat to the left of the driver (who was just to the left of center) and two sat on his right. The unusual cab arrangement enabled him to use the truck both for work and for family transportation, hauling Grandma and two teen-age daughters.

Grandpa finally traded the truck for land on which to build a house, and a subsequent owner apparently thought little of having an extra passenger on his left, for he sawed off the left-side seat. Easily recognized by the off-center shape of its cab, the wide-cab truck was still chugging around Brookings, the county seat and area trading center, when I went off to World War II. If Grandpa had just envisioned installing the additional seating in tandem, he might have stolen a march on the Japanese.

THE DISC GRINDER

A succession of Ts served Grandpa Eichel as family cars and work vehicles. One T was even built into a primitive house vehicle. Perhaps the T with the most lives was the disc grinder which Grandpa developed in the mid-twenties.

The disc grinder had started life as a '22 or '23 touring car. (There was some uncertainty about the year.) Although it had thirty by three-and-one-half-inch clincher tires on demountable rims, the engine had a short oil pan, which made it difficult to reach the rear connecting rod bearing when it needed adjustment.

Grandpa equipped the car with a towing hitch, stripped off the body, and mounted a lathe-like machine on the chassis. The machine was designed to sharpen the blades of disc harrows farmers used in those days to till previously plowed fields for planting oats, barley, wheat and other small grain crops. The drive line was disconnected and the engine belted through a stub shaft to drive the grinder, hence the need for a towing hitch.

Through the early spring months, Grandpa would tour the countryside, bringing his portable disc grinder to farmers' yards and fields, where he could quickly disassemble an implement, sharpen its disc blades, and put it back in service, and the farmer didn't have to take the trouble of dismantling his machine and hauling it to the village blacksmith for sharpening.

When Grandpa died in 1934, the disc grinder was stored in the machine shed. Like most of his possessions, it passed to sons-in-law who could make the best use of them. As the only farming son-in-law, my father took possession of the disc grinder. It was stored in one of the farm buildings. We used it occasionally to sharpen our harrows, but we were not in a position to continue the service circuit Grandpa had developed, and more modern, larger harrows were beyond its capacity. It fell into disuse and was eventually dismantled, but the old T had even more lives.

When my younger brother was born in 1937, Mother's condition required a late-night, high-speed trip to the hospital some 12 or 13 miles away. The trip was too much for the engine of the T sedan that was then serving as the family car. Mother and my new brother were reported doing well the next morning, but the family car had a bad case of loose connecting rod bearings. Rather than tackle a rebuilding job, Dad arranged an engine transplant between the family sedan and the disc grinder. The damaged engine was discarded, and the disc grinder chassis became a trailer to be adapted to a multitude of farm chores.

The disc grinder engine served several more years in the family sedan before the car was replaced by a fancier automobile and the old Ford was cut down into a pickup for farm chores. Eventually the old engine was transplanted again, this time into a T truck that was in regular service for hauling farm loads. It performed faithfully until I parked it in 1942 to go off to help the Seabees in World War II.

When I returned to the farm after the war, the truck had been dismantled and the engine lay in a pile of junk behind the corn crib, along with other discards of more than 20 years of farming operations. Needing something to power a conveyor I was planning to use for loading gravel, I belted the old disc grinder engine to the load and it barked away for yet another summer as I supplemented my GI educational subsidy by hauling gravel to patch township roads and farmers' driveways.

It finally came to an end after it had languished several more years behind the corn crib. A fast-talking cousin told my father that he had an interest in restoring a Model T, persuading him to give him the engine and a considerable accumulation of other T parts. We found out later that he loaded them all up and sold them to the nearest scrap iron dealer on his way back to the city.

MOTOR HOME

Grandpa Eichel was a steam engine man. He ran away from home at the age of 16 and worked for a railroad in Wisconsin. His career was cut short by an accident that cost him the toes of his right foot when he attempted to board a train that was moving too fast.

After he recovered, he packed up his wife and daughters and moved to South Dakota, where he was offered employment running a steam engine for a group of farmers who had banded together to obtain a steam threshing engine. They proposed to hitch it to a gaggle of gang plows

Touring car — Henry and Ida Eichel and their Model T near Oakwood Lakes in South Dakota, about 1919.

Grandpa was a steam engine man — Henry and Ida Eichel look down from the cab of a steam threshing engine at work near Carrington, N.D., in the fall of 1928.

The T became a trailer — The Model T chassis made a commodious trailer for the annual trips to the wheat harvest fields of North Dakota.

Ready to depart — Grandma Ida Eichel and Aunt Nora with trailer ready to leave for North Dakota and the fall threshing season.

and break the prairie sod in three-mile strips.

When the prairies were all plowed, he took up farming on his own; but throughout his life he maintained an interest in steam engines, particularly those used to power threshing rigs.

During the threshing season each fall, he interrupted whatever else he was doing and followed the wheat harvest into North Dakota in a

Motor Home — Grandpa Eichel and the primitive motor home he built on a Model T truck chassis for travel to the wheat harvest fields.

manner that today would cause him to be called a "migrant farm worker."

Early on he owned a vintage teens touring car. Old photos show it with a squared, black radiator, not brass. I remember the rims were permanently mounted to the wheels. For travel, he chopped off the rear seat and replaced it with a box that would hold two bed springs, one on each side, mattresses, a stove, tent, and other paraphernalia necessary for life on the road. You've seen a picture of the rig if you saw John Steinbeck's **Grapes of Wrath.**

That T was later converted into a four-wheeled trailer which could carry a larger collection of camping gear, but for shame, it was pulled by a twenties-vintage Chevrolet. Finally, in the late '20s, the car and trailer were replaced by Grandpa's version of what today would be called a motor home.

It was a primitive living quarters arrangement mounted on a Model T truck chassis. The sides were a lightweight, semi-weatherproof material called "compoboard" (cardboard approximately $\frac{3}{16}$ inch thick) and the roof was canvas stretched over wood bows much in the fashion of the covered wagons that had crossed the plains years earlier.

Furnishings included a full-sized bed, folding table and chairs, kerosene stove, and lantern. Tin buckets and a porcelain enameled pot made do for the niceties of built-in baths and Porta Potties found in modern motor homes.

With the truck and a canvas awning, Grandpa and Grandma Eichel could be at home wherever the harvest season required the services of an engineer to run the steam threshing rig. Every summer, just after the Fourth of July, the house truck would carry him to the wheat fields around Carrington, N.D., where he would be happily employed until the threshing was completed in October and he could head for home.

THE COOKIE WAGON

Grandpa and Grandma Eichel endured some difficult years between the time they gave up trying to farm in 1922 and when Grandpa got a salaried job as superintendent of the County Farm in 1930.

Grandma was an accomplished cook and found work in restaurants in several small towns in the area, but she disliked the hours. For that reason, she went to South Dakota State College in Brookings and completed a short course in dairy procedures to become certified as a ''cream tester.'' With her certificate in hand, she found employment in local cream buying stations.

At one time there had been a creamery in our town that churned and marketed butter made from cream purchased from the local farmers, but its business dropped off when one of the customers found the tail of a mouse in a pound of butter. By the late twenties, the cream was sold to agents who represented cream processing plants in some of the larger cities.

For a time, Grandma worked for A.B. Loomis, the local agent for Hanford's Creamery in Sioux City, Iowa. Later she operated her own cream station for Borden's, also in Sioux City.

It was during Grandma's cream station days that Grandpa acquired one of his most interesting Ford cars. It was a bakery wagon, or peddler's wagon. The body was of wood. It was painted dark green, and the open cargo compartment had curtains of a fabric material like window shades. They pulled down on rollers from the roof of the car, just like window shades, to provide the cargo protection from the weather.

Grandpa acquired the car to perform one of the chores essential to the cream buying business. As the farmers delivered their cream in one- to three- or four-gallon lots (few brought in more than five gallons at a time), Grandma would weigh the can, draw a sample, mix it with a small quantity of acid and run the bottle on a centrifuge for a short period, then read the percentage of butterfat on a graduated scale in the neck of the bottle. After she calculated the amount to be paid for the lot, she would dump it into one of the company cans (ten-gallon cans with the creamery's name painted on the side). She would then wash the farmer's container with very hot water and place it and the check near the door for the farmer to pick up.

At the end of the day, the filled cans were sealed with little wires and lead seals, then taken to the local depot to be placed aboard the freight train, which made its way daily from Sioux City to Watertown, S.D., a distance of about 200 miles.

The southbound train was due in Bruce at about 6:15 p.m., and Grandpa's cookie wagon was just the thing for hauling the cream cans, usually three to six, to the depot each evening. (It was also used to bring back the empties that had been dropped off by the northbound freight on the trip up in the morning.)

My memory is not clear about how long their cream buying career lasted, but I have recollections of Grandma's station being located in at least two places along Main Street and in one storefront on a side street.

Grandpa sold the cookie wagon and bought a '27 T Touring car when times got better.

YOUNG MAN AT THE WHEEL

SUNDAY VISITOR

It was a bright August Sunday in 1931. Almost the entire 270 residents of our little South Dakota town had turned out in Emil Grape's oat field to see an air show. The two World War I type biplanes were the center of attention as they stood parked in the golden stubble of the freshly harvested field. Adults inspected the fabric-covered structures of the wings, fuselage and tail and pondered the wisdom of taking $5 rides. Little boys nine or ten years old were even allowed to climb on the wheels and lower wing step plates.

Near the edge of the field, where the sightseers' cars were parked, there was another center of attention. It was one of those "New Fords," a Model A station wagon. It had a shiny radiator, tan fenders and hood, and a brightly-varnished, natural-colored wood body. Its classy appearance was in sharp contrast to the familiar truck and utility vehicles which, though built with wood-framed, panel-type bodies, were generally painted black or dark green to conceal the grain of the wood and disguise the cheap composition material that the panels were made of.

It was driven by an average-sized, pleasant-looking man dressed in white shirt, creased trousers and dress shoes (also in sharp contrast to the overalls, blue chambray shirts and brogans of the local folks). I assumed he was connected in some way with the airplanes.

I liked his looks, as well as his car, and responded readily to his questions about the location of local establishments such as the school, gas stations, jail, and bank.

We were discussing the condition and connections with main highways of the gravel roads leading from town, when I was summarily pulled away by my father, who sternly chided me for talking too much and said, "That man was asking too many questions!"

With some chagrin, I obeyed his instructions not to talk to him any more, although I didn't see what harm could come from such simple conversation with a man whose car I certainly admired!

I forgot about the incident until Tuesday afternoon, when the bank was robbed! Then, of course, everyone in town speculated about the strangers who had been in town during the air show.

The local constable, "Roy" D.E. (for David Elroy) Perry (no relation to the author) and the county sheriff, Hank Claussen, assisted by some G-men who came from Sioux Falls or Minneapolis, conducted an investigation. Piecing together descriptions provided by the cashier who was accosted and the banker who was forced to open the vault, and with information about other robberies, they decided they knew the identity of the holdup gang. The whole thing was reported in a front-

They don't make them like this anymore — At a tourist restaurant in Florida, the author and daughter Gail inspect a cut down Model T similar to the one he drove when he was growing up on a South Dakota farm.

page story in the *Brookings Press* the next week. There was even a mug shot of the gang leader, the pleasant-looking man with the station wagon. His name was Baby-Face Nelson.

TIRE

At fourteen, I was driving a hand-me-down Model T three miles to school and was also using it to handle chores on the farm. The car had started life as a three-door touring car in 1925. It had worn a succession of bodies, becoming first a ''Tudor coach'' (until the wood in the door frames rotted away) and then a ''Fordor sedan'' before being cut down for its current use.

The cutting down involved chopping off the windshield posts at the level of the lower half of the glass, removing the top, doors, and the back seat. The back seat was replaced by a wood bed, built in the fashion of a wagon box, which rested neatly between the rear fenders to make a pickup truck.

On a bright spring day on the way to or from school (I don't remember which now) I spotted a girl I wanted to impress. I pulled down the gas and accelerated for a maneuver I had seen daredevil drivers perform at the county fair, a high-speed sliding corner.

I yanked the wheel sharply to the left, threw the car into a slide, and poured on the throttle as I corrected to maintain direction. Gravel sprayed and dust flew. I relished the way the old Ford responded. Relished it, that is, until I heard a strange flapping and saw several spectators laughing and pointing to a tire rolling down the road alongside me.

My first thought was that one of the watchers had sent it rolling, but then I wondered who could roll a tire that fast. Then I realized the flapping sound was the inner tube on my right rear wheel. Held to the rim by its valve stem, it was flailing the fender as the wheel revolved.

Air pressure in the old clincher tire had simply not been sufficient to hold the casing on the rim. The slide had torn it from the wheel and let it roll along to overtake me, with the unprotected tube, punctured by gravel, flapping uselessly alongside the naked rim.

The tire itself escaped damage, but it was a long way home on the rim. I was a long time saving $3.25 to replace the ruined inner tube, too. And the young lady took up with another guy who didn't even have a car.

RACE

The handbill read ''Challenge all Comers!'' The event was a Model T race at Midway park in the late '30s. Frustrated because our farm T was laid up with something that couldn't be immediately repaired with bailing wire, my brother and I hitched a ride to the park to view this exciting spectacle.

We were disappointed when we arrived, because there was only one local entry, and it was about to be scratched before the race began.

The local car was a '26 roadster. It had once been one of the fanciest rods in town, with aluminum pistons, Model A carburetor, visored headlights, little red lights on the mud flaps all around, and a Ruxstell two-speed rear axle. Rumor had it that it would do 45 flat-out on a level road.

It had been successively owned by two of the best shade tree mechanics in the community, but as each had grown tired of it and traded for newer, fancier iron, it had fallen on hard times. It was now owned by the town ne'er do well.

Faded in color, stripped of its folding top, and its headlights askew, it sat in the pit area as the traveling participants in the race warmed up their cars and roared through their qualifying laps.

The owner had paid the entry fee, but when he saw the track, he lost his nerve. His supporters had plied him with quantities of his favorite beverage in an effort to bolster his courage, but by the time his courage was up to the task, he was in no condition to drive.

"I'll drive her," I told them, and with the help of several enthusiastic supporters, we began to ready the roadster for the race. We removed the windshield and the glass from the headlights. We unscrewed the exhaust pipe and replaced the Model A carburetor with a standard pot. We considered removing the hood, but the rules forbade it. In short, we threw out everything that wasn't fastened down and took her out on the track for a trial lap.

One thing about the regulars in the race puzzled me. Each car had a leather or web strap or a loop of chain threaded beneath the radiator over the front crossmember of the frame and around the front axle. I was soon to learn what it was for.

The track had been laid out in a pasture with the start/finish line on a level stretch. It bore left into a mud hole down by the river, then came up through a stand of trees and circled back to the start. On the final turn, the promoters had constructed a ramp of planks about two-and-a-half feet high. By jumping over this obstacle, the driver could cut a short distance off the course.

In the qualifying runs, I discovered an advantage. With the Ruxstell in low range, I could roar through the mud without dropping into low as the others did. Then up on the flat I could accelerate faster than those with standard rear end. This brought a howl of protest from the regular drivers. We examined the published rules and argued that despite all the conditions, nothing was said which outlawed the use of two-speed axles. The other drivers finally agreed to let me race, but I would have to start in last place.

The cars lined up, the flag dropped, and we roared away! In the mud, I passed two drivers stomping on the low pedals with all their weight. On the flat, I overtook a couple more and slammed over the jump, hot in pursuit of the leaders. By the end of the fourth lap I was ready to challenge the leaders, but I was beginning to become concerned about the ramp. We were landing awfully hard, and I thought it might be wise to avoid it.

I decided to jump it one more time, which would put me in the lead, and then I could coast home. It was the wrong decision.

As we soared into the air, the nut on the bottom of the spring perch stripped off. The wishbone became detached, the front axle dropped, and the car vaulted over the front wheels, making a wide circle in the direction of the crowd. It finally came to rest with its nose buried in the soft pasture. I flew over the useless steering wheel, slid off the hood, and tore the seat out of my yellow corduroy pants.

I didn't know it at the time, but my mother's sister was among the spectators. By the time I had hitched a ride home, Mother and Dad

Lyle and me — I was sixteen months older than Lyle. Mother dressed us as a pair of model children.

had a complete report. I never did get to use the story I cooked up to explain my torn britches.

LYLE LEARNS TO DRIVE

The left front fender of the old T had obviously been dented. It had been straightened as best it could be with farm tools, but it unmistakably showed evidence of a mishap. This dent was the result of a collision with a cow in a 35-acre pasture where 34 cattle grazed regularly. Across this acreage ran the farm road that led to the south fields of the farm we worked when I was growing up. With an acre for each bovine and one left over, the pasture should have provided room enough for a driving lesson, but it did not.

Lyle was about a year and a half younger than I, but it was difficult to convince him of that fact. From the time we were six or seven, we were the same size; and what I did, he did also. It was the same with learning to drive. In fact he got a head start, for he was allowed to drive the tractor that pulled a two-row cultivator, while I had to run a single-row plow pulled by a pair of mules.

There was a difference, however. Although he did steer the tractor between the rows of corn, Dad rode the converted horse-drawn cultivator and operated the pedals that steered the implement's shovels along the rows of young plants. To insure that Lyle didn't let the outfit run out of control, Dad fastened a pulley to the tractor frame and led a rope from the clutch pedal through the sheave and back to his seat so he could bring the machine to a halt if Lyle's steering went awry. Lyle was probably nine at the time.

I did get to drive the Ford first, however, and I was soon driving it to and from the fields like an old hand. Lyle insisted on being allowed to learn to drive too, so one bright summer day, as we were on the way back from the south fields, we stopped to open the pasture gate and I let him slide under the wheel and drive through the gate. I chased the cows that had gathered in hopes of getting into the adjoining cornfield, and waited to close the gate behind him.

As he inched through the gate, one roan cow persisted in trying to get through the opening. With the low pedal depressed, the car was moving slowly, and Lyle expected the cow to yield as the car approached. She did not. When he saw that she could not be bluffed out of the way, he became flustered and released the low pedal, intending to stop. But he had already moved the hand brake forward; and when he released

What I did, Lyle did — Sometimes mother dressed us alike. Picture was taken in the summer of 1926.

the low pedal, the transmission went directly into high gear. The Ford leapt ahead, striking the startled cow on the rear as she bellowed in fright and ran.

Damage to the cow was hard to determine. At least it healed. The T bore the scars for the rest of its service life.

THE WRECK OF THE HAY RAKE

It was a bright July day, a good day for making hay. That is exactly what we were doing — my father, my younger brother, Uncle Len, and me. For some reason we needed a hay rake from the farm operated by my uncles, about a half mile away across the fields and a short distance down the road.

To save time, I was dispatched to get it in the Model T farm vehicle, a cut-down car with a box on the back like a pickup truck. I was 13 or 14 at the time and had just learned to drive.

With my uncle's help, I lifted the tongue of the rake into the bed of the vehicle and then fastened a chain between the trailer hitch (mounted to the shackle bolts of the rear spring) and the draw pin on the rake. We headed for home.

I was careful getting onto the road. I inched though the driveway gate, and with more than a quarter mile of straight dirt road across the field, I eased the gas lever down a little and headed for the farmyard gate. Too late I realized that with the tongue of the rake riding at the right side of the box, the rake was tracking a good two to three feet to the right of center, and I was steering right at the middle of the gate.

The rake was 12 feet wide, the gate 14 feet. At best I would have a foot of clearance at each side. Trailing off-center as it was, the rake was going to miss by at least a foot.

I stood on the brake, to no avail. With six feet of slack chain between rake and car, the rake just kept coming. Its tongue slammed against the back of the seat just before the right wheel caught the fence brace a foot outside the gatepost. The rake slewed sideways and the post broke off at ground level; the tongue crashed against the side of the truck and broke off at the roots. Then the right wheel bent outward as the wreckage was dragged through the opening. It was a disaster.

The time-saving effort of fetching the rake with the Model T turned into a half-day session of repairing the broken tongue, straightening the bent wheel, and replacing the gate post.

The tongue even looked rather neat, spliced and splinted with a couple of broken hay bucker teeth, but I never could admire the repair job without embarrassment.

SHIFTING THE WARFORD

Of all the add-ons sold for the Model T, perhaps the most nefarious was the Warford transmission, which was installed in T trucks to provide extra gearing for hills and heavy loads. This device was widely known as a killer, and for good reason. Automotive lore abounded with horror stories about drivers killed or maimed by that transmission.

I remember hearing my Grandma Eichel comment to Grandpa about "that old Warford," but I didn't understand her feeling that truck owners who installed them were stupid. Then when Carl Hovey rolled his truckload of oats upside down halfway up the Bruce hill, I was puzzled as to why the transmission was blamed for the mishap.

I was to learn the secret when I got big enough to drive the T that Dad acquired for use on the farm when I was 12 or 13 years old.

The truck had been purchased in the mid-twenties by "Doc" Perso, a well-to-do neighbor who traded it in on an early V8. Although its ancestry had been certified when Dad bought it, there had been some modifications. It was identified as a '24 or '25 model, but the engine was equipped with a carburetor that appeared to be '26 or '27, and it had the wide foot pedals for the low and brake that identified it as a '27.

It had been fitted with the Warford auxiliary transmission, a three-speed unit in an aluminum case that provided a super-low gear for hills and heavy loads, a direct drive for ordinary running, and an overdrive for high-speed running empty. I soon learned the reason for Grandma's apprehension. The unit mounted directly behind the planetary transmission, which was integral with the T engine. When the Warford was in neutral, the rear wheels were not connected to the major braking

You load "Sixteen Tons" and you get a flat tire! — Model TT truck being loaded with gravel at Aurora, S.D., in summer of 1923. Capacity of truck was slightly more than one cubic yard.

system, a friction band in the primary transmission. The only braking available when the Warford was out of gear was the relatively ineffective rear wheel "emergency" brakes, controlled by the hand brake lever, which disengaged the clutch when it was pulled.

With no brakes and no help from the engine, a loaded truck rolling backward downhill was nearly impossible to control. The best of drivers could not cope with the tendency of the front wheels to cramp, causing the vehicle to overturn, and more often than not sending it rolling over and over.

The Warford was not synchronized. Shifting it with the truck in motion required a skill for double clutching that few farm drivers ever mastered. That operation was made doubly difficult by the fact that the speed of the engine was controlled by the gas lever on the right-hand side of the steering column. This meant that the same hand had to regulate engine speed and simultaneously shift the gears.

Dad's first admonition when I drove the truck was, "Never try to shift the Warford into low gear when the truck is moving. Always stop and shift into low before starting up a hill!"

As soon as I was allowed to tinker with it, I fitted the engine with a foot-operated accelerator and was shortly double-clutching and shifting the Warford with a skill that would be a credit to the jockey of a modern-day eighteen-wheeler.

As you might expect, I grew overconfident. One day when I was breezing absentmindedly along, I became aware of the need to shift down. Too late to take advantage of the truck's momentum, I missed low gear and stalled and, to my horror, began to roll backward downhill with the Warford in neutral.

I held the steering wheel rigidly and tried desperately to jam the lever into gear. The gear teeth clashing against each other jarred my wrist painfully, but even using all the strength I had, I was unable to force the transmission into gear.

The shift lever protruded through the floor just ahead of the seat, slanting slightly forward to provide clearance for the gear positions. Low gear was straight forward. I put my right foot on the lever and my left on the reverse pedal and then stood on the shift lever.

Leg-strength carried the day. The transmission made a noise like the case was splitting in half, but it went in gear. I jammed down the reverse pedal. The engine spun furiously with a gasping sound. As it caught and roared, I, in as much of one motion as I could manage, got off the reverse pedal, jammed down the low pedal, and pulled down the gas. The backward motion slowed, then stopped; and finally the truck began to inch up the grade. I did the rest of the hill with the low pedal hard on the floor and the gas lever all the way down.

I continued to drive the old T doing farm chores until I left for the Seabees in 1942, but I certainly was a lot more careful about shifting after that.

DRIVING TO SCHOOL

ELSIE HITS THE WIRE

For those of us who lived on farms during the 1930s, driving to high school was no big deal. We learned to drive as a necessity to help with farm chores, and drove to school whatever vehicle the family could make available. On any given day, there would be a half dozen cars parked at the edge of the street in front of the village school.

The usuals were Swede Anderson's '28 Model A, Byron Winkleman's '31 A, Bill Ford's '32 Chevy, the Hovey twins' '25 Buick sedan (or a late-teens Dodge sedan which they had cut down into an open-topped pickup), and a couple of '37 Fords driven by Marvel "Bud" Jefferis and Glenn Krulish.

The "town kids" walked to school. Few had access to cars. An exception was the banker's daughter, who drove her father's late model Dodges (which were renewed every other year or so).

A tradition developed that the guys taught their girlfriends to drive. The only problem was that there were not enough guys with cars.

Family (if not school) rules dictated that the cars be driven only to and from school and remain parked during the day except for special reasons. On early spring days, most of us found some special reasons to drive a bit during the lunch hour.

It was during one of these special excursions from the school to downtown Bruce (about four blocks) that Swede agreed to let Elsie drive. She may have had some wheel time in her father's '26 Model T, but she had never driven a car with a clutch and gear shift on the floor.

Swede explained the process: push in the clutch, shift into first, let out the clutch, accelerate a bit, push in the clutch, shift into second, let out the clutch, shift into high, etc., etc. For stopping, push in the clutch, shift to neutral, step on the brakes. Elsie did fine all the way to main street and back, but when she turned to park (heading into the sidewalk in front of the school where there was no curb) she got all mixed up.

She pushed in the clutch and the car didn't stop. She let out the clutch and pushed the brake. It still didn't stop. In panic, she pushed down on all the pedals and killed the engine just as the bumper hit the guy wire that held the pole carrying telephone wires to the school.

The pole bent as the wire stretched like a bow string. Then it snapped, about five feet above the ground. Pulled by the wires at right angles to the building, it fell away from the car; and although the car escaped damage, Elsie's composure was shattered.

The start of classes was delayed as all 102 students from the first grade up ran out to see the "wreck." Elsic fled to the girls' rest room, leaving a red-faced Swede to explain to the principal how the accident had happened, and to his steady girl friend, Nadine, how Elsie had come to be driving his car.

Fellow students had a great time preparing an official-looking phone company statement, listing damages of $25 to replace the pole and restore service. However, the principal (who at first agreed to go along with the gag) changed his mind when he saw the stricken look on Elsie's face.

OTTO de CRATE

Otto de Crate was a 1926 or '27 vintage Buick sedan. It had been named by its owner, Mr. Thomas Rice, the whimsical young man who taught music and English in our small high school and courted the Methodist minister's eldest daughter.

By the late thirties when Mr. Rice and Otto showed up at our high school, Otto lumbered and wheezed. The song of its gears had dropped from a musical whine to an uneasy growl; and when the going was tough, it became a positive groan. On hot days, the red column of mercury in the thermometer on its radiator cap edged awfully close to the danger mark.

Although Otto's worn snubbers sometimes allowed its wheels to thump into the chuckholes in the gravel roads of South Dakota, its paint was still shiny and its upholstery was respectable. The varnish on the yellow wood spokes of its artillery wheels still glistened. It had character.

Mr. Rice and Otto were popular in the school and in town. Otto's commodious seats could carry the teacher and at least seven young people to the school and church events that made up the social life of our little community. On trips to basketball games in the neighboring towns, there was never a shortage of passengers. Mr. Rice willingly piloted Otto on these excursions; and more than once, I hitched rides as an extra

The ghost of Otto de Crate? — Bill Sanders inspects a 1925 Buick during a recent visit to Florida.

passenger when otherwise I would have been left stranded.

It was on one of these basketball trips that Otto came to a crashing end. We were playing in the finals on the second night of the conference basketball tournament in Estelline, another small town about ten miles to the north. For the first night's play, plans had been carefully laid and schedules arranged to enable most of the student fans to attend the games. Otto and its master were pressed into service to transport a load of fans.

Since we were far from assured of a berth in the finals, arrangements for the second night were less structured. Only hours before tip-off, several students were still looking for a ride to the game. Mr. Rice had a commitment somewhere else and could not be available to drive Otto to take students to the game.

Whatever Mr. Rice was doing that evening did not involve Otto, and the car remained parked behind the house where Mr. Rice was boarding. Moreover, one of the fans, a young man who had been a star on the team the year before, knew about a little quirk in Otto's makeup. The ignition switch could be locked and unlocked with a key, but if it were left in the unlocked position, the key wasn't needed. The ignition switch on the dash would turn the ignition on and off.

As the game time approached and it became clear no other ride was available, the fans hatched a plan to "borrow" Otto. The young man who knew about Otto's switch knew how to drive. They scouted the parked vehicle and ascertained that both Otto's doors and ignition were unlocked, so eight of them packed in and they were off.

At the county line, eight miles north of town, the highway made two right-angle turns to correct for a mismatch in the section lines that had occurred when the two counties were surveyed. The first turn was to the left; and slightly more than a quarter mile farther, the second was to the right. To facilitate travel, the curves had been graded on an easy radius and banked so they could be negotiated at 40 miles an hour. (A skilled driver could probably make it through at 45 with a little sliding.)

We were nearing the end of the winter, but there were still a few icy spots left on the road. One of them was on the inside lane of the first turn.

At the precise moment that Otto and its load of teenage basketball fans was being steered carefully around the outside lane of the first curve, two farm boys with reputations for reckless actions approached the curve, from the opposite direction, in a pickup truck. There was plenty of room to pass, but for some reason the driver of the pickup lost control.

The truck struck Otto just ahead of the hub on the left front wheel. The axle took most of the shock, but the succeeding sideswipe ripped off both doors and spilled the teenage passengers out onto the road. Miraculously, no one was badly injured, although there were a few superficial scrapes and bruises. After being picked up by passing motorists and checked over by the local doctor, most went on to the game.

Otto was towed home the following day, its left side completely ripped away, the tire and rim from the demolished front wheel thrown in among its dislodged seat cushions and broken doors.

Spectators clucked over the narrow escape our young people had. The fact that they probably had no business driving Otto on that ill-fated trip was overlooked in the swell of relief that they had not been harmed. One of the Hovey twins who had an artistic bent was commissioned to draw a picture of the wreck; it was reproduced in the mimeographed school newspaper.

Through the efforts of the insurance companies involved and some of the students' parents, Otto was replaced by a Buick sedan of similar vintage, but it was not the same. The sound of the replacement car's gears was different, and it had spindly wire wheels. It simply wasn't Otto! The romance was gone.

In epilogue, Mr. Rice married the preacher's daughter and they bought a new car for their honeymoon. On a less happy note, the young man who drove Otto on that fateful night was killed some years later in a late-night crash on a highway in Wisconsin, where he had gone to seek employment.

SKIP DAY

One of the traditions of my high school days was senior skip day. As a reward for 12 years of diligent study, the school sponsored a one-day outing by members of the senior class to whatever metropolitan attraction the class treasury could finance.

Our class elected to attend the Dakota Relays, a prestigious Midwest regional track and field meet held annually at Sioux Falls. (The idea probably originated with our coach, because it provided a way to finance participation in the meet by a team that appeared to have good prospects in a sprint medley event.)

The team was comprised of Marvel (alternately called "Bud" or "Jeff") Jefferis, Charles Gheringer, Robert Schutzer, and myself.

I was the only senior. During the track season, Jeff and I had qualified for participation in the state finals in the half-mile and mile races, where we ran just out of the money. I was delighted to have one more race opportunity.

Since grade school days, Jeff and I had lived on neighboring farms not quite three miles from school. We walked or ran back and forth to school. With the routine of regular farm work, we didn't need much of a program of physical conditioning. The other two team members were also farm boys, and although unseasoned in competition, both were able to run a 220 in the low twenties. My best time in the quarter-mile was under a minute, and Jeff could do a half-mile in just under two minutes. We were ready.

We set out in three cars. In addition to coach's new 1940 Chevy two door, Jim Beam drove his father's '33 Ford V8, and Roy Rassmusen took his brother's recently-acquired '35 Chevy. (Roy's older brother Herman had bought the car only a couple of weeks earlier at a fantastic price of $225. Although nearly five years old, it looked good and the engine had just been overhauled. A mechanic friend had gone over it carefully and pronounced it an excellent buy, although the amount was a lot for a young married couple.)

Roy was paired (not yet quite engaged) with Elsie. A girl named Alice, related to Roy through marriage and in whom I had more than a casual interest, was also a member of the class.

We set off on a bright May morning, planning to arrive in time for lunch, then spend a leisurely afternoon and have dinner before the evening session of the relays. All went according to plan except that two cars, Jim Beam's '33 Ford and Roy Rassmusen's '35 Chevy, had not arrived by lunch time. After some delay we ate, somberly apprehensive about what had delayed the rest of the group. The athletes had been promised steaks at lunch, with the expectation they would eat lightly at dinner before the race. I offered to share mine with Alice, but she was worried (her sister was Roy's brother's wife).

It was well after mid-afternoon when the missing cars showed up. The Ford, boiling furiously, was towing the Chevy with a length of barbed wire scrounged from a farmer's fence.

Details remain a little uncertain, but somewhere south of Dell Rapids, about 25 miles from their destination, and in an attempt to make up time lost in dalliance or just teen-age drivers' poor judgment, the two cars were racing along near the limits for that vintage iron. In fact, it was more than the limit for the Chevy. Elsie, who felt responsible for Roy, recounted:

"As Roy had sped past the Ford at nearly 70 (and it took a good Chevy to hit 70 in those days), there was a sickening explosion, followed by terrible noises as the car came to a stop.

"When they lifted the hood, they found a hole bigger then a man's fist in the side of the motor block, through which they could see the cap of a connecting rod. It had come loose from its mounting bolts on one side and was folded back against the main part of another rod, which had been forced through the side of the engine. The new car, the skip day outing, and probably even the relay meet were ruined!

"The rest of the trip was a nightmare. We had to find something to tow with and wait for the Ford to cool at intervals."

Jeff had borne the brunt of the ordeal. Although not one of the drivers, he had taken the lead in rigging the tow, in deciding when to rest the boiling Ford, and in holding the group to their purpose to press on to the meet. Although relieved to have arrived, he was worn out.

The gloom was heavy as we gathered around the disabled Chevy and the boiled-over Ford and told ourselves that we couldn't let the incident upset the athletes and spoil our chances for a good race.

The reassurances had little effect. As we waited for someone from home to pick up the stranded students, we spent a dispirited afternoon in the stands watching performances by some of the best athletes in the Midwest. We theorized that the mechanic who had overhauled the Chevy had left the cotter key out of a connecting rod bolt. (After having learned about engines and mechanics, I now rather think he had clamped a rod bearing too tightly on a slightly out-of-round crank journal, a common Chevy ailment and a common mechanic error. The engine might have survived under normal driving conditions, but it was not up to the strain of 70 mile an hour driving.)

Alice felt responsible because she had interceded with her sister to allow her brother-in-law to let Roy drive the car. I tried to remain detached as I dressed for the race and limbered up on the cinder track, but I could not escape a feeling of vexation.

Our event was called. I dug into my starting holes. I was always a fast starter, and that night I got one of my best. I held my position down the backstretch and, pouring on a sprint at the finish, I vented my frustration at the day's events on the other runners as I raced by them. My teammates came through, too; Jeff was unchallenged in the final lap. Our time was a record which stood for more than 20 years.

Roy died during World War II. The last time I saw his brother Herman, some 45 years later, he had forgotten the car and the incident.

MISHAP

I had my first accident while driving a borrowed car, and it cost me a good share of my summer's wages.

Five of us farm boys had driven to Sioux Falls in Don Haroldson's car to attend the Sioux Empire Fair. The car was a '35 Chevy two-door that his father, a farmer who was somewhat more prosperous than the rest of us, had bought for Don to drive to high school.

We had a good day at the fair, but there was this girl I knew who lived in Sioux Falls. Through the course of the day I telephoned her and made a date to take her to the grandstand show that evening.

I borrowed Don's car and drove to her home as if I knew the big town like the back of my hand. A pretty, round-faced blonde with large brown eyes, she climbed in beside me. I had met her the winter before, when we both worked night jobs at the college in Brookings.

As we set out for the fairgrounds on the west side of town, I had to drive against the sun. I don't know whether it was the sun, the large truck that blocked my view of a traffic light, or the fact that I was paying more attention to the girl than to driving. My first hint of trouble came when I saw her gasp and point to the truck directly in front of us.

Traffic had come to a halt at a red light, and the truck had stopped directly in front of our car. I stood on the brakes, but it was too late. The car skidded under the rear of the truck, smashing the grille, breaking one headlight, and knocking the other askew. My date was thrown from her seat but, fortunately, was not injured.

We both did our best to pretend it was no big thing, but I don't remember anything more about the date, the grandstand show, or getting her back home. I do remember having to tell Don I had wrecked his car, and I'll never forget our long drive back home with only one headlight and the fender rubbing on the tire every time the car steered to the right.

Back home, we assessed the damage. The grille would have to be replaced. We figured $50. A new headlight lens and straightening the fender would add $25 to $35. I told Don I would take the car to Brookings to a body shop.

I did, and the estimates astounded me. One friendly body man showed me that the grille shell and both front fenders had been pushed back nearly three quarters of an inch by the impact, and the contours of the fenders where they bolted to the body near the firewall were distorted. He explained that it would be necessary to disassemble the whole front clip in order to pull them forward and back into shape.

He wanted $250 to fix the car. I had been earning $2.50 a day at farm work for the summer and I had saved about $285. I haggled as hard as I could and we finally settled for $200.

It was an expensive date.

MY FIRST CAR

The first car I bought and owned on my own was a 1930 Chevy sedan. I had first seen the car about six months earlier, when a neighbor's son (whom most considered lacking in good judgment) blew his summer's wages to acquire it. He then spent most of what he earned to buy gas, not to mention certain other liquids he consumed as he cut a wide swath through several of the neighboring towns.

Eventually, the fate the neighbors had predicted befell him. More precisely, he ran into a farmer's cow on a country road in the wee hours of a Sunday morning, killing the cow and considerably damaging the front end of the Chevy.

The car was towed to Commodore Roy's junk yard, where I spotted it on my way to town. Curious, I stopped to examine it. The left front fender was smashed, a headlight was broken, and the radiator was knocked askew.

Not in complete seriousness, I asked the Commodore what he would take for it. He said $25.00. I asked about a fender and some parts for the front end, and he pointed to a similar car in the lot with an undamaged fender.

"$2.50 for the fender and headlight," he said. "You take'em off."

"How about $20 for the car and fender?" I inquired.

We settled on $22.50 for the car and the parts, and I towed it home to the farm.

In short order I replaced the fender, straightened the radiator, and had it running. However, there was a problem. It made four tracks in the driveway, for it ran crabwise down the road. My father and other jeering observers attributed the problem to a bent frame, which in their eyes made the car useless. (That had been the diagnosis when the original owner had towed it in and sold it for salvage.)

I found however, that the bolt in the center of the right rear spring was sheared off, and the rear axle was out of position by at least two inches. With that repaired, it came much closer to alignment.

After that, I drove it up beside the granary and carefully measured distances from several points on the chassis to the foundation of the building (a relatively straight line for reference). I concluded that the chassis was still about a half inch out of alignment, so I moved it forward until the front end extended past the corner of the granary up to the cowl. With some iron stakes and heavy timber, I staked down the rear end, fitted a block between the frame and the foundation of the building, and hitched our heaviest tractor to the front end with a chain, to pull sideways to the left around the corner of the building.

After a couple of tugs and more measuring, I concluded I should quit before I introduced a cant in the opposite direction. I released the Chevy from her chains and put her on the road with a slight adjustment of the tie rod to correct toe-in. The rear wheels now followed the front, and my reputation as a mechanic began to spread.

I continued to drive the Chevy comfortably and safely until the following fall when I enlisted in the Seabees and entrusted it to my younger brother, who drove it to high school for three years. When he came of enlistment age, he parked it behind the granary where it rested until I was discharged the next winter and returned to reclaim it.

By that time, I was driving a much sportier Ford convertible and had no use for the Chevy, but I hauled it out, fired it up, and offered it for sale. It wasn't long before someone who needed a car offered to trade his broken-down vehicle for one that would run. I demanded some boot (naturally), patched up the trade-in, and traded again. Within a few months I had traded five times, winding up with the same car and $350 in cash.

It had spent some time in the possession of a young farmer who was dubbed "Cocky Doodle Doo" by the neighbors. You can guess the reasons. The sounds from the engine suggested loose connecting rods.

I replaced the engine with one I had purchased for $15 from a farmer who was making a trailer of his Chevy, and sold the car again for $85.

DOWN ON THE FARM

UNCLE LEN BUYS A CAR

Dad's brother "Len" was my favorite uncle. It wasn't only because I looked like him. A shy man with a quiet manner, Uncle Len could spin a yarn with the best of them when he was at ease with the family or with friends he knew well.

He would balance on the back legs of his chair, making distressing indentations in Grandma Perry's kitchen linoleum. Cradling his pipe, or whittling aimlessly on a piece of wood with a pocket knife kept razor-sharp, he would tell about horses, farming, hunting, and all kinds of adventures.

An explosion in a German ammunition dump in World War I had left his hearing impaired. A tangle with the husking rollers of a corn picker one cold winter day had left him without full use of his right hand. He could cradle his pipe and wield his whittling knife, but the index finger on that hand always extended straight out in a useless fashion.

The oldest of a family of six boys and five girls left fatherless by a tree-cutting accident when he was in his late teens, Len shouldered a lifetime burden of looking out for his mother. He was unschooled and could barely read newspaper headlines, but he understood farm work, and he raised beautiful horses.

In addition to the accident that killed Grandpa Perry, another personal accident affected Len's life and his outlook. A severe blow on the back of his head, received when he drove under a neighbor's manure carrier while helping with threshing, nearly ended his life in his late 20s.

The blow resulted in a subdural hematoma (a blood clot) which created pressure on his brain, causing disorientation and loss of memory. Shortly after the accident, family members noticed that he was acting "funny." When they could no longer manage his unpredictable behavior, they arranged for him to be hospitalized in the VA Center at Marion, Ill. Although he was able to walk and talk, he was unaware of his surroundings or of what was happening as he was driven to the hospital.

To everyone's surprise, he regained consciousness more than a year later and rapidly recovered. He returned to farm with his bachelor brother and their mother, later moving to a farm just across the road from our place.

Because of his disabilities, Len received a small veteran's pension. It provided the major support for his bachelor brother and their widowed mother when the crops were poor or the prices low.

During the moneyless days of the early thirties, a shirttail relative who had spent his life avoiding working at a job took a brief fling at selling cars. Uncle Len was a prime prospect as a customer. He had a regular income and he didn't own a car, but there was one drawback: He didn't know how to drive.

The relative offered to sell him a used Essex, and as part of the deal, he would teach him to drive. After a couple of lessons, Uncle Len was able to start, stop, shift, and steer well enough to drive from the farmyard to the nearby fields. All went well for nearly a week.

I was 14 or 15 at the time and had just graduated from the Model T (with its three pedals) to the clutch and shift of Grandpa Eichel's '29 Chevy. I rode with Uncle Len and monitored his performance, cautioning him to brake occasionally, making certain he steered to avoid a troublesome gatepost that had been set in the middle of the lane that provided entrance to two fields.

The trouble came when he decided to drive alone to the west quarter, a half-mile down the road and across the railroad tracks.

I looked up from something I was doing in the shop to see Uncle Len walking up the driveway. He had come for my help to get "that damn car out of the fence." We set out, not in the direction of his farmyard, but toward the railroad crossing about a half mile west. I could not see the car because of tall corn in the field, but I grew increasingly apprehensive as Uncle Len muttered about the train, brakes, and steering wheel.

I found the car at the far side of the road, a good block before the railroad crossing. It was sitting at an angle with the front bumper tangled in the woven wire of a hog yard fence.

Apparently unnerved when the train crossed his path, Uncle Len had lost track of the pedals and was unable to bring the car under control. It had swerved off the road, traveled across the shallow ditch, and come to rest in the fence. There appeared to be no damage to the Essex, but the wire was stretched a little out of shape.

With him holding the wire away from the bumper, I was able to back the car out of the fence and drive it out of the ditch. With it safely back on the road, I moved over for him to take the driver's seat, but he adamantly refused, saying, "I'm never going to drive that damn thing again!"

He didn't. Until he retired from the farm, he traveled back and forth to town with his two black mares and a triple box wagon that had been fitted with wheels and tires from a discarded automobile. The flashy black mares were spirited runners. When he took the "farm road" that ran through the fields along the railroad track, he could make it from the farm to town as fast as anybody could drive the two-and-a-half miles of gravel road that followed the farm borders. He never again felt the need to learn to drive.

A LOAD OF SWEET CLOVER SEED

Uncle Bruce's clover field was going to seed. It was late in the summer of 1942. In those days, the government farm program included payment for taking land out of cash grain production and planting it with legumes, on the theory that the grain surplus would be reduced and the land would be renewed by the legumes, which put nitrogen back into the soil.

The program allowed farmers to harvest the legumes for livestock feed, and although alfalfa made the best hay, many farmers opted for sweet clover because it was easier to grow and the clover made good hay if it was cut before it got too big.

That's exactly what happened to about 40 acres of Uncle Bruce's clover. Since it got too tall to make good hay before he got around to mowing it, he decided to let it head out and then harvest it for seed.

It was a disaster. When it ripened, the clover was about the texture of willow brush. We struggled for days getting it cut and tied into bundles, using a binder that constantly stalled when the tough stems wrapped around any rotating shaft that was unprotected. Threshing it was no easier. When the clover dried, the seed shattered from the stalks at the slightest movement, and the separator had to be carefully adjusted to keep from blowing the small seed away with the chaff and straw.

We finally got a load of 50 or 60 bushels, which I hauled to town in the Model T truck.

Proprietors at two of the town's three elevators would purchase the clover seed, and at Uncle Bruce's suggestion I took it to the one that was part of a large chain operated out of the county seat. This suited me, because the manager's daughter, a classmate of mine, was almost engaged to my best friend, Roy.

We chugged onto the scales and weighed the load. The elevator man took a sample of the seed for testing. The testing device shook the seed in a stream of air through a series of screens into a stack of three drawers. The top drawer collected the chaff and bits of stalk that were too large for the screen and too heavy to be blown away. Clean seed was collected in the lower drawer; the contents of the middle drawer consisted of seed with the hulls still on, heavy enough to fall through the screen, but too large to sift into the clean seed drawer.

The contents of the middle drawer were then placed in a scarifier, which knocked the hulls off and blew them away, leaving an additional quantity of clean seed.

I watched as the elevator operator weighed the contents of the lower drawer and recorded the amount. Next he weighed the good seed recovered from the scarifying process and noted it beneath the first amount. He then subtracted the second amount from the first and used the result to calculate the percentage of good seed in the total sample.

I thought he had made an error and told him I though he should have added the two amounts of clean seed to determine the percentage. He assured me that he was following the procedure prescribed by his home office, and that he always did it that way. I insisted the calculation made no sense.

The argument quickly developed into a shouting match. I was convinced I was right; and at 19, I was brash enough to make an issue of it. He yelled that he had been buying grain all his life, and no damn kid was going to tell him how to run his business.

In a huff, I drove to the next elevator which was only a half block down the railroad tracks. The attendant was reluctant to test the load. He had heard some of the shouting and didn't want to get involved. He finally agreed, however, and, following a procedure that simply made an estimate of the seed to be recovered without actually going through the scarifying process, came up with a result which, while better than the one I had argued about, was still not as good as I had come up with when I followed what I believed to be the correct procedures in calculating the results of the earlier test.

In frustration, I drove the truck home, parked it in the driveway of the granary, and confided the details of the dispute to Uncle Bruce and my father. They decided Uncle Bruce would have to negotiate the sale of the seed himself and that it would be best to wait until tempers cooled.

The load was still parked in the granary a couple of weeks later when I left for California and the service. I learned, long after, that a retest had come up with a result less favorable than the one I had turned down and that Uncle Bruce had sold it without protest.

There was another unexpected and far reaching consequence of the incident, however. My challenge had left the elevator operator in a foul mood. He went home and ordered his daughter to cease keeping company with my friend Roy. That night Roy and Elsie eloped.

ALEX DRIVES TO TOWN

Alex, who farmed across the road from my father in the years after I left the farm, was a pretty casual farmer. His small row-crop tractor ran for years with only one front wheel. Since he seldom applied grease — I don't know whether he lost the grease gun or if it just ran empty — the bearing in one wheel wore out. Instead of repairing it, Alex simply removed the wheel and operated the tractor without it.

His car offered evidence of a similar approach. In the early forties, he was driving a Dodge open touring car from the late twenties or early thirties. It was not surprising that it looked like one of those vehicles John Steinbeck's Okies left behind when they moved to California.

Since the radiator leaked badly, Alex didn't bother with anti-freeze. He simply filled it with water when he was going somewhere and refilled it when a cloud of steam signaled it was necessary. It froze in the fall and remained frozen until spring.

With only a few chores to occupy his winter days, Alex liked to drive into town in the afternoons and play euchre with other similarly occupied farmers at Ray's pool hall. With its radiator frozen, the old Dodge would make only about a mile and a half of the two miles to town before it would overheat and stall. At this point, Alex would leave it at the side of the road and walk the rest of the way into town, where he would spend the afternoon at cards.

By the time he was ready to return home, the engine had cooled sufficiently to start again, and he would walk back to the car, start it up, and drive home.

In 1949 he bought a new Dodge, and for a couple of years, the routine changed. The new car could make it all the way to town and back.

Eventually, however, the new Dodge wore out. When it was replaced by another, it was parked in the woods between the house and the field, just back from the main road. It stood there, neglected, for years.

During threshing one fall, my younger brother (then about seven or eight years old) and a neighbor lad of the same age were tagging along with the threshing crew from farm to farm. Exploring the farmyard, they amused themselves by playing driver in the abandoned car. In the course of their play, one of them opened the glove compartment and, to their surprise, found a check for more than $1,300. Fearing they had gotten into something they shouldn't have, they put it back and forgot about it.

Later, during the winter as Dad and my brother were driving to town, my brother caught sight of the car through the bare trees and remembered the check.

"There's a lot of money in that old car," he said to Dad.

Thinking he was referring to a possible antique value of the car, Dad scoffed until my brother recounted finding the check.

In short order, Dad brought it to Alex's attention, and sure enough, in the glove compartment of the rotting hulk of a car, they found a check issued by the soil conservation service for more than $1,300. It was Alex's government subsidy for not farming part of his land in the years of crop surpluses.

"Hell," Alex said, when he found the check, "I must have forgotten about it!"

Despite his casual methods, Alex left his only daughter 320 acres of good South Dakota river bottomland which served well to attract potential husbands.

OFF TO COLLEGE

A JOB'S A JOB

Like many of my generation, with World War II looming on the horizon, I had begun to work my way through college before military service and the GI Bill insured my educational opportunities.

It was no big deal. Tuition at South Dakota State College was $17.50 a quarter, and room and board could be had for $5 a week. The $.25 per hour I earned at a couple of part-time jobs enabled me to meet my bills, and I was having fun.

On weekend evenings, I served as a busboy at the Rainbow Cafe for my meals, 21 hours for 21 meals. On Monday and Tuesday mornings and on Saturdays, I worked for Jack Horner's speedy delivery service, driving a Harley 74 and an assortment of beat-up pickup and panel trucks to deliver groceries, coal, ice, hot water, and occasionally more interesting packages.

Some people think I'm putting them on, but hot water was the mainstay of the business. The water supplied by the municipal water system was laden with minerals. It was so hard that, in those days before the Culligan salt-pellet household water softening system, even using Ma Perkins' best Oxydol, housewives found it difficult to whip up suds in the washing machine.

Because the water-hardening minerals also corroded the boilers and clogged the pipes, the city light plant installed a softening system to treat the water used in the generating system. My boss made a deal with officials at the light plant to buy hot, softened water for five cents per ten gallons. They installed a spigot in a little shed at the back of the plant where we could run the water into ten-gallon milk cans, which we then delivered to laundry tubs of the women of the community at fifteen cents a can, or two cans for a quarter.

We developed customers on a regular route, which we serviced on Monday and Tuesday mornings. Jack and I, and another full-time driver, would begin at 4:00 a.m., with six cans loaded in the motorcycle sidecar and eight in a pickup, and go as fast as we could until about 10:30, when all the washing machines in town were filled and churning out laundry.

PACKAGE DELIVERY

There was more to delivery service than hot water; the package delivery business provided some entertaining moments.

Jack's "fleet" consisted of a '36 Dodge pickup (a fine machine used only for light errands and the water run), the Harley, a battered '37 or '38 International three-quarter ton truck, and a very tired '34 International panel truck. Navis, the full-time driver who was engagcd to the boss's daughter, regularly drove the Dodge. Jack drove the International pickup or rode the Harley, and (while I liked the excitement of the motorcycle and was partial to the Dodge) I drove anything that wasn't on the street when I came to work.

I learned to walk with a swinging gait that enabled me to carry a ten-gallon can of scalding water in each hand without burning my legs against the hot cans.

On Wednesday morning we delivered groceries for a store that still took orders by telephone, and on Friday we delivered ice and hauled coal, ashes, or trash. Throughout the week, Jack's wife took phone orders for incidental package deliveries and dispatched us on errands as they came up.

It was one of these incidental errands that lent spice to the job. One rainy morning, I was sent to a Second Street address to pick up a package to deliver to the campus. When I arrived at the address, a pretty blonde girl ran out and jumped in the truck.

"Where's the package?" I inquired.

"Me," she giggled. "I'm the package."

I looked at her uncomprehendingly.

"But we don't deliver people," I stammered.

"Look," she said, "It's raining and I need to go to class. The taxi will charge me a quarter. You deliver packages all over town for a dime. Deliver me to Old North Hall."

When I hesitated, she held out her notebook.

"Here," she said, "I want this notebook delivered to Old North Hall. A girl named Esther needs it. I'll just ride along to see she gets it."

"But your name is Esther," I said, looking at the name on the front of the book.

She smiled and seated herself on the upturned pop crate that served as an emergency seat in the rickety old panel truck (which had only a seat for the driver). She was young and pretty, so why should I argue?

She became a regular customer after that. On rainy mornings she would call, and sometimes, knowing her class schedule, I wouldn't wait for her call. I usually tried to insure that I was driving the Dodge or at least had something for her to sit on when I picked her up.

WAGES

Wages when I was a kid didn't amount to much. For farm work as a teenager, I earned $2.50 a day for such heavy labor as pitching bundles or scooping grain for a threshing rig.

When I went off to college I earned $.25 an hour cleaning up in a restaurant and driving a delivery truck.

In October of 1942 I found myself in the Rivera section of Los Angeles enlisted in the U.S. Navy Seabees but assigned to inactive duty and subject to call on a 24-hour notice. It was a pleasant place to be. My girlfriend worked for Douglas Aircraft just down the Lakewood Expressway, but there was a problem. I was out of money.

Expecting the Navy to call me immediately upon enlistment, I had spent my summer's earnings on traveling and entertaining my girl. Now I would have to go to work. I stopped at the only business establishment in town that looked like there were live people around to make inquiries. It was a general blacksmith and auto repair shop, servicing tractors, trucks, automobiles, and farm machines used in the nearby orange groves.

In response to my inquiry about work, the proprietor removed a stub of a cigar and asked:

"Can you weld?"

I told him I could.

"There's a job laid out in the back room," he said. "Let's see if you can do it."

The job was a four-foot section of drag harrow used to work the soil between the orange trees. Several of the teeth were damaged or missing. A nail keg held a supply of new teeth, which were to be welded to the frame. I counted the teeth. There were enough to replace the whole lot. I fired a cutting torch and cut all the old teeth off and then arc-welded new ones in their place. When I had finished I had a harrow that with a little paint would have passed for new. I took it to the front of the shop and threw it down in front of the boss.

He chewed his cigar as he inspected it.

"Looks pretty good," he said. "How much you want?"

Back home I had worked for $2.50 a day. My co-worker at the delivery service, who was engaged to the owner's daughter, was paid $15 a week. The most generous salary I'd heard of till that time was $25 a week.

I hesitated, trying to make up my mind whether I had the guts to ask for $25 a week.

Before I could respond, he said, "I'll give you thirty bucks a week. Take it or leave it."

SMART-ALECK TRUCK DRIVER

As the farm prospered, the TT truck was replaced by a two-year-old '36 Chevy that was to serve the farm for years after I had gone.

Whatever cargo body the truck had carried had been transferred to its successor by its former owner, and the truck arrived at the farm wearing nothing but the cab on its naked chassis.

My brothers and I helped Dad build a combination grain box and stock rack that was an object of pride. The floor was laid of two-inch, quarter-sawn, straight-grained fir planks, with ship-lap edges for a grain-tight platform that would provide years of smooth shoveling. The stakes were two-inch white oak, and the sides were tongue-and-grooved fir flooring. The sides were bound with iron fittings made from a pair of discarded drill wheel tires. It was one of the few truck bodies in our community suitable for hauling flax seed, a slippery commodity that would flow almost like water.

I drove the truck lovingly, glorying in the sound of its smooth six-cylinder engine and solicitously double clutching as I shifted the gears up and down to match the load and grade. I loved the exhaust note the engine emitted when it was holding back a load in second gear.

I took the joy of truck driving with me when I enlisted in the Seabees, and the first detail I was assigned to when we landed on the South Pacific island of Tongatabu was driving a pair of tankers that supplied the base with water from a government-maintained well near the center of the island. I had two 1941 Chevy trucks with 900-gallon tanks. At the base water tank, I connected a hose, started the pump, and roared off to fill the other truck while the loaded one was being emptied. When the tank was emptied and pressure dropped, power to the pump was shut off until I returned with another load. Shuttling both trucks back and forth throughout the day, I was able to supply the 18 to 20 thousand gallons of water the camp used each day.

As I came from chow one evening, barely after having the routine established, I encountered a fellow Seabee who was having difficulty with his task. He had been assigned a tank truck similar to those I drove, but it was used to transport diesel fuel from piles of drums stored in the jungle to the fleet of mine sweepers and submarine chasers berthed in the harbor. A likeable—but totally incompetent—seaman, he was unable to master the routine necessary to insert a two-inch suction line into a barrel of diesel fuel, drain enough from the tank to prime the line and maintain the prime as he shifted the valves to pump fuel from each drum. He had been working all day and had not been able to get his truck loaded. He asked if I would go with him to help make the pump work. I agreed.

It was early evening when we returned to camp with a load of fuel. My intention was to return to my quonset hut barracks and let the hapless driver deliver the load to the two sub chasers at the dock. As I dismounted from the truck, the skipper's yeoman, an officious, sawed-off Italian with political ambitions, came charging from the company office yelling, "Where the hell have you been with that truck? They've been waiting for that fuel since mid-afternoon!"

There may have been more, or it may just have been the way he said it, but since it wasn't my detail, and I didn't like being yelled at, and because I was bigger than he was anyway, I chased him back into the office.

It was a mistake. The company had another tank truck. It was called the "honey wagon," and it was used to pump out the holding tanks for the latrines and haul the contents to the far end of the island where they were dumped into the Pacific. (Although we weren't particularly environmentally conscious, we told ourselves it was the Japanese side of the ocean.) Guess what my next detail was!

There was a sequel to the fuel story that was far more significant than the nasty reassignment I drew. That night, as the sub chasers were dispatched on an emergency mission, both stalled out with water in their fuel.

Investigation the next day revealed we had loaded fuel from the wrong pile of drums. Drums in the pile we drew from contained fuel salvaged from the battleship South Dakota after it had run aground in the channel at the entrance to our harbor. It was known to have been contaminated with sea water and was intended to be used only for burning in water heaters and stoves on the base.

I was never able to determine whether the fuel truck driver had been given the wrong instructions or if the mistake was caused by additional incompetence on his part. The captain's yeoman made certain I shared the blame.

SHOWING OFF

Despite the "honey wagon," I continued to enjoy driving trucks; and when we were loading ship, I drew extra duty driving trucks that delivered cargo to the docks. During one late-night detail, as I worked a two-ton Dodge stake bed down through the gears to slow for the pier entrance, the skipper remarked to Pop Fields, the very soft-spoken motor mac who maintained our trucks, "There comes Perry again, I can tell it's him a mile away!"

A fellow Seabee, who told me about it later, was surprised at the intensity with which Pop responded to what he apparently considered criticism of my driving. "Yes sir, but don't complain about Perry's driving. He's the only driver we've got who's never tore up a truck in the two years we've been on this island!"

I did come close, however. One evening, as we collectively fought off boredom, I was showing off my skill at backing a truck, gauging my progress by watching the road in front of me. I had bet I could back a semi-trailer crash truck a half mile without looking back. I almost made it, but I had forgotten the road past the base forked at the edge of the camp and there was a tree in the middle of the fork. A resounding crash ended my bet and brought several Seabees running to see what had happened. Fortunately the truck was built to withstand rough usage, but the scarred tree served as a reminder of my lost bet until we shipped out!

Another time I came close to destroying Pop's faith in me, I was heading back to the well for another load of water. The route took me something over a mile along the beach to the center of Nukualofa, where it made a left turn and led straight inland for about three miles to the turn-off to the right for the well, which was another three-quarters of a mile up the hill.

Leaving Nukualofa, I passed an Army six by six loaded with supplies. It was driven by an untidy looking dogface. Three or four native workers were seated on the crates and boxes in the back. The man waved in a desultory manner as I passed, shifted into second, and gunned the Chevy to road speed, about 50 or 55 miles an hour.

At the turn-off, I slowed and started to turn across the road. Despite the fact that we drove on the left side of the road in Tonga, a British protectorate, no one had bothered to put rear view mirrors on the right-hand side of our trucks.

As I started to turn, a terrible racket came through the open right window. It was a combination of roaring Jimmy engine, squealing brakes, and plaintive beeping of a military courtesy horn. Although I had not given him a thought after I passed him, the Army driver had been pushing his cumbersome truck to its limit in a futile attempt to race my empty Chevy. He caught up with me as I slowed, but he realized too late that I intended to turn across the road in front of him. I was not even aware he was there.

I swung the Chevy back into my own lane just as the bumper on the front of the Army truck grazed the side wall of my rear tire and watched as the loaded cargo truck veered off the right side of the road, through a slight ditch, and into an unoccupied grass hut at the roadside. Groceries, palm fronds, and Kinakis were flying everywhere.

I stopped the truck and ran to see if anyone was hurt.

"I'm sorry," I said, "I didn't know you were there."

The soldier retrieved his cigarette from the floorboard of his truck, pulled his cap back on, and said:

"Geez, I didn't know you wuz gonna turn!"

Fortunately, no one was injured, and the native workers were all big grins and excitement as they packed the spilled cargo back into the truck.

Pop did have to replace the tire, but he didn't lose faith in me, and he put right-hand mirrors on both my trucks.

CANDY BAR

An amusing incident that had nothing to do with driving occurred while I was hauling water for the camp. On one trip I picked up a New Zealand soldier who was hitchhiking back to his camp across the island from our base. For some reason I also had another rider who occupied the passenger seat in the cab, and the soldier volunteered to stand on the running board on the driver's side.

In a burst of generosity, I stopped at the canteen at the edge of camp and bought a handful of candy bars, giving one to the passenger next to me and one to the soldier on the running board. Both immediately tore off the wrappers and started eating. Some moments later, when I had the truck moving down the road and shifted through the gears, I opened the wrapper on the O'Henry bar I had bought for myself. I withdrew the cardboard strip from the bottom of the wrapper and threw it out the window.

I was not prepared for the soldier's reaction. An embarrassed look spread over his homely face and his eyes seemed to come together as they focused on what remained of the candy bar he was eating.

"Blimey," he said, "I thought it was bloody tough chewing."

He had eaten the candy bar, cardboard strip and all.

CLIFF'S NEW CAR

Among the most memorable of my college experiences are the trips I took with the forensic squad. There was red-haired Gladys, tiny blonde Mavis with the brown eyes, and willowy Jean with dark hair and deep blue eyes, who danced so easily . . . but this story is about cars.

With a natural gift of gab (my uncle Bill called me "Windy"), and with a penchant for righteously speaking out against what I thought was wrong with the world, I was recruited by the debate coach as a freshman. And during my upper class years, I became one of the regulars on the eight-person squad of debaters. I also doubled in competition as an extemporaneous speaker. (My coach often chided me for speaking extemporaneously in formal debates.)

Our team was nationally ranked, and we traveled from Denver to Cleveland, Fargo, Peoria, and Oklahoma City (brief hops by air today, but in those days we traveled in the coach's car and whatever other automobile we could enlist).

On one jaunt to a national competition at Bowling Green State University in Ohio, we drove the coach's '40 Chevy (which at 100,000 plus miles had just undergone an engine transplant) and Cliff Hullinger's brand new '46 Ford Tudor.

Cliff, an older student, was a veteran of World War II, attending college on the G.I. Bill. Asserting his status as a veteran to get his name at the top of his hometown Ford dealer's waiting list for cars, he had plunked down $1,400 of his savings from his Army pay for one of the first available cars.

A beauty it was—light beige with matching upholstery and plastic trim. I noted when we left the campus the odometer read 43 miles.

When we were barely out of town, Cliff offered to let others share the driving, a gesture which we chalked up to his being a nice guy with pride in his new car. Since we both itched to get at the wheel of such a classy vehicle, B.J. Sauber and I took turns that were just short of "hogging" the show and drove most of the 900 miles to Ohio.

Cliff didn't even seem overly apprehensive when we got caught in a downpour in the Chicago area and raced from route to route, attempting to find one that had not been closed by the flash flood the rain had created. At one juncture we inched through water that covered the highway to a depth of eight or ten inches, behind Bob Moorman, who had taken off his shoes and was wading along the side of the road, feeling the edge of the pavement with his feet.

While we were rescuing a young woman who had climbed on top of her submerged car (which she had driven into the ditch when the road took an unexpected turn), a highway crew arrived and began marking the road with stakes driven into the shoulder.

The rest of the trip was without incident until we approached the Chicago area on the return trip. In those days before Interstate highways, U.S. 6 swept right through downtown Chicago. Although Cliff had indicated he wanted me or B.J. to drive through the downtown area, we had not found a convenient place to change drivers, and before we were aware of it, we were caught up in the city traffic with Cliff at the wheel.

Not being familiar with the route, Cliff was determined to follow the coach closely and not to lose him in the heavy traffic. Our coach, being familiar with the city and its streets from his years as a student at Northwestern University, charged through the traffic like a veteran cab driver.

Cliff followed grimly, braking and accelerating wildly to avoid being cut off and losing him in the melee. At one point he dodged left through an opening between a streetcar and the support pillar for the elevated, that appeared to be no more than inches wider than the Ford. From the back seat, I could see the motorman's startled face looking down at me through the rear window. The trolley's gong sounded against the back of my head.

After about 40 minutes of what seemed like bumper cars on a midway, traffic thinned to a point where we were proceeding uninterrupted, with the coach's car in easy view ahead of us. The other passengers and I breathed a collective sigh of relief. We had escaped with our lives, and the new car had survived without a scratch. Cliff lifted his hat, wiped perspiration from his brow, and said:

"I didn't tell you this, but I learned to drive after I got this car!"

NO DOWN PAYMENT

MY FIRST V8

I purchased my first V8 for $165 in East Greenwich, Rhode Island, while I was awaiting discharge from the Seabees after my return from the Pacific at the end of World War II.

It was a black '34 Ford coupe with bright red wheels (poppy red, the restoration manuals call it today). I really wanted a Chevy. I had grown up with Chevys, had owned one before the war, and had driven GMC and Chevy military trucks all through the war. I was convinced that V8s were tinny, burned oil, wasted gas, and were altogether less satisfactory than Chevys.

But with thousands of returning GIs looking to buy cars, I thought I was lucky to find such a beauty. The upholstery was good, there were no dents, and the tires had good tread.

The engine made a sound like my mother's sewing machine. Later, when I had learned about V8s, I realized that the sound signaled a very worn engine; but in comparison to the tappet-rackety Chevys I was used to, it was quiet.

I did notice it smoked, and I asked about oil consumption, but the guy selling it said it hadn't been run for some time, and he had put oil in the cylinders when he got it out of storage. He said it would clear up as the car was driven. It seemed like a good explanation, so I counted out his money and drove away in a cloud of blue smoke.

I drove the car for a week with no lessening of the smoke. In fact, if it didn't get any worse, it did become more embarrassing. When I drove away from a stop light, the next two cars in line had to wait for the air to clear before they could find the way.

The next week, as I was breezing along the highway toward Kingston, I thought there was really less smoke behind me. I began to believe what the man had told me. Then I heard a different sound from the engine. It was definitely a rattle. I looked at the dashboard gauges. A separate oil pressure gauge had been mounted under the dash. It showed satisfactory oil pressure. Nothing else appeared wrong.

I stopped the engine, got out, and lifted the hood. The dipstick showed not a trace of oil. I wiped it off, thrust it back in place, and withdrew it again. Still no trace of oil. I wondered what damage I might have done to the engine as I walked a mile or so to a filling station and bought four quarts of oil. I figured that would get me going again, and besides, it was about all I could carry.

I poured it into the engine and cranked it up. It sounded no worse than before, and I looked at the oil gauge with satisfaction—it still showed oil pressure.

Then a thought hit me. I shut the engine off again and turned the switch back on without starting the engine. I still had oil pressure. I turned the switch off. The needle dropped. Back on, the needle rose again even though the engine was not running. A quick check of the circuitry showed the oil pressure gauge was wired to the switch rather than to the sending unit in the engine block. It registered satisfactory oil pressure any time the switch was on.

That afternoon, I posted a note on the bulletin board at the base entrance: "For sale: '34 Ford coupe, looks great, runs good: $175." I sold it that evening to a sailor who had been discharged and was going home. He offered $165. I didn't quibble. I hoped he lived in California.

TRADING CARS

When I got home from the service, the '30 Chevy which I had left with my brother was parked behind the granary. He had driven it to high school for a couple of years; but as the war dragged on, its tires wore thin and gasoline became scarce. He had parked it, and the family had made do with only one car from then on.

I had bought a much newer Ford convertible and no longer had any use for the Chevy, but with the demand for cars as great as it was, I thought I might be able to sell it. I gassed it up, pumped up the tires, and drove it enough to satisfy myself that it still ran. Then I passed the word that I had a car for sale.

A young man from town, a Navy veteran like myself, offered to trade me a '36 Olds, but there was a catch. His car didn't run. The bearing in the water pump had worn so badly that the fan had run out of position and destroyed the radiator.

I wasn't certain I could repair his car. Parts were hard to come by, and finding a radiator would be impossible. It was a newer car, though, and I thought perhaps I could get something to boot. I can't remember for certain, but I think I asked for $150 and settled for $125.

Then I set about getting the Oldsmobile running. I found a radiator from a Chevy. It had less capacity than the one on the Olds, but it would bolt in place. The water pump was another problem. The bronze bushing had worn completely away, and the shaft had worn into the pump housing so far that it would have been impossible to fit a new bushing, even if one had been available.

I removed the pump from the engine, clamped it in a bench vise, and centered the shaft in the hole as best I could "eyeball it." Then I melted some babbitt and poured it into the recess around the shaft. When it cooled, I had a perfectly fitting bearing. I improvised a seal with some oil-soaked cotton string, the way we often packed the shaft on a Model T. It didn't leak.

Although I could now drive the car, the radiator was still a problem. It would overheat quickly, since the core of the Chevy unit was too small.

A fast-talking friend who was making a business of buying and selling cars soon noticed that I had the Olds running, and he proposed a trade for a '33 Chevy he was driving. I drove his car. It seemed okay, although the transmission was noisy and the speedometer did not register. He explained that it had been necessary to replace a broken cluster gear; so with little quibbling, we settled on a deal that gave me $60 to boot.

As I drove the car for a few days, I saw that the speedometer cable housing was hanging under the chassis, and I became convinced that the noise I was hearing came from lack of lubrication in the transmission. I resolved to check the oil level. As I crawled under the car to reattach the speedometer cable, I discovered it would not be necessary to check the lubricant in the transmission. There wasn't any. There was a hole the size of a dollar in the transmission case.

I decided I could patch the hole, so I carefully cut a piece of sheet metal to cover it. After drilling three holes and threading them to take quarter-inch bolts, I fastened the patch over the hole with cap screws and a gasket cut from an old felt hat. With the repair completed, I drove to town to fill up the transmission with new grease.

With the job finished, I started to back off the grease rack. Within a few feet, the car stopped abruptly, as if it had encountered an obstacle. I shifted gears and let it roll forward a bit. In reverse, it again halted after a few feet; but I let the clutch all the way out, and it seemed to crunch over whatever the obstruction was. I drove home without incident.

As I walked away from the car at home, I saw oil dripping underneath. I looked. The patch I had carefully placed on the transmission case had been pushed away, tearing out one of the mounting holes I had drilled, and the reason was obvious. Something had been wedged between the gear on the countershaft and the transmission case. As the gear rotated, it had been forced through the side of the case. A thorough flushing of the transmission case with kerosene turned up a tooth from the broken cluster gear that had been left in the grease when the gear had been replaced. With the transmission dry, it had rested harmlessly in the bottom of the case. When I filled the unit with grease, it was picked up by the gear and forced out through the side. I concluded it had probably been the cause of the original hole.

A new patch, not quite as neat as the first because of the destruction of one of the mounting holes, sealed the case so it would again hold grease. The transmission sounded much better from then on.

Shortly after that, I sold the car for $225 in a neighboring town to a trader who never bothered to look at the underside.

A short time later I had an opportunity to buy another car, the same '30 Chevy I had started with. It had been traded a couple of times since I sold it, and a previous owner had dressed it up with mud flaps and trinkets, but he had driven it hard. It was suffering from a bad case of loose bearings (something not uncommon among splash-oiled Chevys that were driven hard).

He asked $75. Figuring that I could quiet the motor and sell it again, I offered $50; we settled for $60. I returned home with the car I had started with, having gained a total of $350 along the way. I was on a roll, but the end was coming. New cars were being delivered daily, and old heaps were less and less in demand. By the time I had replaced the engine with one I bought for $15, I was barely able to recover my money. I traded it for a broken-down Terraplane that had lost its clutch. No parts were available for it, and I wound up selling it to a farmer for $35; he made a farm wagon trailer from the chassis.

While I was swapping and selling cars on my own, I made contact with a sharpshooter in the county seat who operated a used car lot. He offered me a commission on any of his cars I could peddle. I managed to swing a couple of reasonable deals for friends who relied on my knowledge of cars to make a good selection for them, but I was embarrassed that one required an expensive brake overhaul that I had not expected. Another resulted in a tragedy that is the subject of another story. I gave up trying to deal with this sharpshooter when he sold a friend of mine a '35 Plymouth that broke down before he got it off the lot. When, after repeated complaints, my friend was unable either to get his money back or get the car fixed, he threatened to leave it sitting near the dealer's entrance as a warning to prospective customers.

"You bought it; now get it out of here, or I'll charge you storage on it," the sharpshooter told him.

THE CAR I WISH I HADN'T SOLD

The car I wish I had never sold involved a question of to whom it was sold, not a case of a vehicle I wish I had kept.

Richard "Dickie" McElliot was a muddle-witted, spoiled son of a domineering woman who was better at business than at mothering. Through at least three marriages and some hard work, she wound up owning the most successful cafe in town.

Dickie blundered along in school until the draft caught up with him. He somehow survived the war and came home to live with Mother, across the street from my home.

His mother asked me to help Dickie find a good car. Price wasn't a great concern, she said; she would pay for it, but she wanted him to have a "safe" car.

I figured the safest vehicle to let Dickie drive would be a wheelbarrow, and I wouldn't be too confident of that. I told my wife I was reluctant to become involved because the young man was so irresponsible.

"He'll just go out and kill himself or someone else," I predicted.

I brushed off his mother's follow-up inquires with excuses that I hadn't found a car that would be a good deal for them. Finally, after some weeks had passed, she informed me that Dickie was going to get a car that week and that if I couldn't find one for him, someone else would. Against my better judgment, I brought home a nice '36 Ford Fordor.

The car looked good. It ran well, and the interior was not worn. It needed brake work, which I insisted the dealer's mechanic take care of before I would show it. In spite of this, it was indeed the best vehicle I could find.

They bought it and Dickie drove it a week. The following weekend he got drunk at the veterans club and started for Brookings. Nine miles north of town, he sideswiped a new Pontiac, driven by a pair of local youths, and kept on going. The pair turned around and pursued him. A high-speed chase ensued.

When he crested a small hill about three miles from town, Dickie lost control of the Ford. As the car skidded sideways, the right rear tire blew and the car mowed down a swath of fence-post-sized ash trees before coming to rest in a farmer's grove.

Dickie survived the accident, but he was paralyzed from the neck down. He has spent his last 35 years driving a wheelchair in a veterans hospital. When my wife and I made a courtesy visit to the hospital on the day after the accident, we were barred by the mother, who screamed, "It would never have happened if you hadn't sold him that damned car!"

STEERING WHEEL LOCK

SHOWING OFF

My college chum Gil Zeman tells this Ford story on himself. He grew up on a farm and learned to drive the family Model A at an early age.

As a teenager, he was pretty confident of his driving skills. He developed a habit of rolling up the driveway, making a left turn, and coasting to a stop in the usual parking space beside the granary.

He became so proficient at it that he would depress the clutch, shut off the ignition, and roll to a stop in just the right place with only a light touch on the brake. To show off, he would withdraw the ignition key and drop it in his pocket.

When the family bought a new '37 V8, he practiced the maneuver with the new car. One day he came rolling up the drive, aimed for the parking spot, and shut off the engine. Without thinking, he snapped

A bit of nostalgia — The 1935 Ford Cabriolet driven by the author during his college days sparked his current project to restore a similar car.

A new '35? — The author poses with a restored Ford Cabriolet owned by Hugh Freeman of Fairview, N.C.

Shall we start over? — A similar 1935 Ford Cabriolet for restoration was located near Montreal in 1987.

the ignition lock, withdrew the key, and dropped it into his pocket—and crashed into the corner of the granary. He had forgotten that the steering column lock served both the ignition and the steering.

WINDSHIELD

The ignition switch on the '35 Cabriolet I bought after World War II had been converted from the original key and toggle lever on the steering column to a push-pull on the dash. I wasn't happy with that arrangement. Since the doors didn't lock, anyone who knew which button to pull could drive the car away.

The toggle lever had been removed; but the bolt that locked the steering column remained in place, although it appeared to be wedged in the unlocked position. There was the possibility that it could still lock the steering, but since it had not been a source of trouble for me yet, I ignored it. There wasn't much else I could do. Replacing the switch on the steering column seemed a difficult task, and since I was a college student at the time, my resources were limited. I drove it for a couple of years without incident.

One spring day, as I was heading down a country road on my way to class, I noted a pheasant rooster in the fence row. He leapt into flight directly in front of me, and my first reaction was that he was just in time to clear the car. We both misjudged. He rose slowly, directly in front of me, and I soon realized that he was going to hit the windshield. I ducked my head to the right as he smashed into the glass and came crashing through in a shower of splinters.

He went over my shoulder and landed on the back of the seat, fatally injured and bleeding on my new seat covers. I opened the door and let him fall out onto the road and then turned to assess the damage.

The windshield had a hole in it a foot in diameter. My right hand, which had been at the top of the wheel, was scratched and bleeding slightly, and I felt a trickle of blood on the left side of my neck just below my ear. There was glass everywhere.

Avoiding the wind coming through the broken windshield, and holding a handkerchief to my bleeding neck, I drove on to the campus and checked into the student health center for a Band-Aid.

I was offered a seat which I accepted, still holding the hanky to my wound. Sensing that I was in some distress, a pretty nurse came to determine the extent of my injury. She inquired about the cause.

As I recounted the accident to her, she ran her hand through my hair.

(I had thick wavy locks then.) Then she moved over to the wastebasket and brushed off a handful of loose hair and glass splinters. Only then did I realize how fortunate I had been.

A previous owner of the car, during wartime, had replaced the windshield with one-fourth inch plate glass. When it broke, it shattered into a million pieces. Although I had ducked at just the right instant to avoid getting a face full of glass splinters, a shard the size of a pocketknife had passed through my hair, cutting a swath as neatly as a razor would have done it.

I took the car to the local body shop to have the windshield replaced. It cost me $18. The amount was modest, but I wasn't totally pleased. Because it was an old car, some of the screws were rusty and difficult to remove, and the body man hadn't bothered to remove the instrument panel. He had simply pried it out of the way while installing the new glass and then banged it back in place with a rubber hammer. I didn't like his repair methods; but since I considered myself lucky to have escaped serious injury and had anticipated a bill twice the amount, I accepted his workmanship without complaining.

On Thursday evening of the same week, I was driving on a washboarded country road. I rounded a big curve at about 45 miles an hour. As I came out of the curve, I was surprised to find I couldn't turn the wheel. The locking bolt in the steering column (which I have earlier described as inoperative and jammed in the unlocked position) had been jarred free, either by the hammering windshield repair or the washboard road, or both. It had jiggled into a position which locked the steering!

The car continued in a circle, tearing out great chunks of road shoulder as it dove off an embankment, crossed a wide ditch, crashed through a fence, and finally stopped in a grove of small trees.

There were two strands of barbed wire at the top of the fence. When the car went through them, one strand broke somewhere to the right, the other to the left. I watched helplessly as they raked across the front of my car, one going one way and one the other. Barbs caught the hood ornament, breaking it off, sending it flying through the air directly in front of my face, smashing my windshield again!

AN ASSEMBLED CAR

THE GREEN COUPE

I purchased my third V8 as a result of a disaster in my life. The car, too, was a disaster.

I had driven the '35 Cabriolet for nearly five years. Although I had maintained it regularly, it was beginning to fray. The history of the car before I owned it was somewhat uncertain, but there was evidence that the odometer, which was creeping up on 100,000 miles, might be on its third trip around.

I faced medical bills that were mounting every day. My assets were a modest trailer house and the car. My only recourse was to sell the car, and since it was a convertible and still looked sporty, I reasoned that it would bring a good price if the buyer didn't look too closely at the signs of wear.

Only a year or so earlier, I had turned down an offer for considerably more than the car had cost new, because I knew that I would not be able to replace it for that amount and because I really liked it.

Ignoring the obviously chauvinistic implications, I left the car with my brother-in-law, who lived near an Indian reservation. I told him to sell it to some Indian at an outrageous price. It sold, much as I expected it would, but that's another story. A co-worker and good friend, who also liked the car, bought it and brought it back to town.

Meanwhile, I had seen in an alley not far from where I was living a tired-looking '37 coupe that had not been moved for months and had no license plate. (I later learned there was a reason.) Deciding the car was unused, I thought if I could get it cheaply enough, I could make do with it until my finances improved.

I inquired at the front of the house. "Is that old car out back for sale?"

I was directed to the rear of the house, where a rangy, uncombed, and mostly unwashed individual was languidly engaged in some chore, working with somewhat less enthusiasm than he was expending on his ample chew of tobacco.

I repeated my inquiry. The man spat and replied:

"Yep."

"How much do you want?" I asked.

"Seventy-five dollars."

I made as if to look the vehicle over. I'd already seen the worn tires and the faded paint.

"Does it run?" I asked.

"Yeh," he replied, refreshing his chew from a rolled up paper pouch. "It runs real well."

"Can I hear it?" I asked as I twisted the hood ornament and struggled to lift the hood.

"It hain't got no battery," said the owner.

He explained that he worked in a carnival. The season had been bad and he was "laid up" at home and needed money more than he needed the car.

I looked at the gutted interior; the headliner and door panels were gone. The seat, done in brown leatherette, although well worn, was surprisingly not torn or broken down. The radiator showed evidence of a rusty fluid, and the dipstick dripped a nasty black oil. Beneath the faded paint, the body and fenders appeared smooth and unblemished. It was surprising that the car could have survived the kind of abuse it had obviously been subjected to without acquiring some dents.

I kicked one of the bald tires and said, "I'll give you fifty dollars."

"You got cash?" the man asked.

"Sure," I said, reaching into my pocket.

He spat again and we made a deal.

As I was preparing to tow it away he volunteered, "Hit ain't got any rod out, neither."

The remark surprised me, because I had accepted his assurances that the engine was sound.

He was lying. I discovered that fact as soon as I cranked it up, but I was prepared to do some engine repair. I tore it down and measured the crankshaft with a borrowed micrometer. The journal that carried the worn out insert was between five and six thousandths out of round. A neighborhood mechanic advised me that "If you don't can it, you can get away with running a new insert on that journal."

I took his advice and reassembled the engine with new connecting rod inserts. He may have been right. The engine sounded good, and I drove it gingerly.

I undertook to replace the missing headliner with one I made from some monk's cloth I bought for a couple of bucks from the remnant counter at the local dry goods store. I also repaired the door panels with brown imitation leather that came close to matching the seat. After investing another dollar in a can of wax, I had it looking and running like a "respectable car."

All went well for two or three months. Then one day as I was breezing down the highway, I was startled by a tremendous *bang!* Immediately everything in front of me went black. Some moments passed before I realized that the hood had come unlatched and had folded itself neatly over the top of the car.

Using only a pair of pliers, I was able to detach the bent-up hood and stow it in the trunk, but now I was late. To make up time, I pushed the hoodless vehicle up near the 70 mark for the remaining 10 miles into town, which was a mistake. When I let up at the edge of town, the roar of the engine changed to the distinctive pecking sound of a knocked-out connecting rod.

I drove home slowly, pulled the engine, and removed the oil pan. The new bearing insert had broken into half-inch fragments and was falling out of position under the dual connecting rods. There was now no question about it: the crankshaft would have to be replaced.

THE BLACK TUDOR

Since early spring, I had noticed a nice '37 Tudor parked in the same spot on a side street I passed each day. Somehow I had learned that the owner carelessly had failed to protect the car with anti-freeze during the winter and it had a hopelessly cracked block. Hoping it might provide a replacement crankshaft, I inquired of the owner if he would sell me the engine. He offered me the whole car for $45.

I couldn't believe my good fortune. The car looked like new. The paint was black and shiny, and the upholstery showed little wear; all it needed was an engine. I could replace the broken block with the block from my ruined engine.

I consigned my tired coupe to the junkyard and set about building an engine from the parts at hand. The product sounded good. I drove it to Minneapolis. On the slightly less than 500-mile round trip, I added seven quarts of oil.

I took stock and decided this car was good enough to merit spending some money for repairs. I could get a remanufactured engine from the local Ford garage for $225. For less than $300 total investment, I would have a nice car.

I bought the engine, installed it, and again drove to Minneapolis. (It was a nearly disastrous trip in a freezing winter snowstorm, which is another story.) To my dismay, the rebuilt engine was noisier than the one I had discarded, although this time I added only three-and-one-half quarts of oil. I complained to the dealer.

"Well," he told me, "sometimes these engines take a while to break in. Drive it a thousand miles and let the rings seat. It will quiet down and quit using oil."

I drove it a thousand miles. It was still noisy and still used oil. Now he told me that sometimes they take a little longer to break in.

"Drive it another thousand miles, and we'll see if it doesn't get better," he said.

I drove it another thousand, then two thousand. It was still rattling and still used oil. I returned to the dealer to renew my complaint.

Sitting in front of his showroom was a nice '42, six-cylinder Tudor. He suggested that since my engine was unsatisfactory, rather than replace it, he would make me a good deal on a trade. I agreed and drove it home, out another $216. What the hell?

CHEVY HAS "BEE" ACTION

Grandma often used the phrase "put a bee in her bonnet" when she wanted to urge someone to action. I got an indication of what she was suggesting one day while driving my brother's '35 Chevy coupe.

It was a hot August day in South Dakota. I was breezing along the flat road that led along the Sioux River bottom between Brookings and Volga. I had both windows rolled down, and to encourage a breeze through the car, I had turned the somewhat generous vent windows around until they functioned as wind scoops to direct air into the car. The wind felt good on my face.

Air wasn't all they directed in. Traveling at something over 50 miles an hour, I encountered a large black mass floating across the roadway at windshield height. It was a swarm of bees.

I swerved but could not avoid it. Hundreds of bees smashed against the windshield directly in front of my eyes. The driver's side window vent scooped additional hundreds into the car right in my face. Many went by my head and piled up on the package shelf between the seat back and the rear window.

The bees and I were both stunned momentarily, but not for long. The car was soon alive with black bodies crawling in every direction in search of a way out of the trap into which they had been swept. I could hear their ominous buzzing over the sounds of the wind and engine.

I shut off the ignition, reached for the emergency brake, and pulled it on hard. Then I opened the suicide door and stepped out onto the running board, happy to leave the car to the bees.

After bringing the car to a stop, I stood back at what I considered a safe distance and surveyed the disaster. To my amazement, although several bees had hit me squarely in the face, I had not been stung. The bees, as they recovered from the impact, began to look for a way out of the car. I opened both doors and helped as many as I could with sweeping motions of a straw hat I had placed on the seat beside me. As soon as they were out of the car, they flew off in the direction they had been going when I hit them. In a matter of minutes they were all gone except for a few that had been killed by the impact. I gingerly brushed them from the ledge and seat before driving on.

WITH AUTOMATIC TRANSMISSION

SHIFTING THE HYDRAMATIC

The '49 Mercury is credited with establishing the pattern now used universally for the shifting quadrant for the column-mounted automatic transmission lever (P-R-N-Dr-Lo). My first Oldsmobile with a hydramatic had a different order, N-Dr-Lo-R. Reverse was used for parking, and the stop pawl would not lock in if the car was moving above a predetermined speed. In addition, in order to shift into reverse (which was at the bottom of the shift lever travel), it was necessary to pull the lever slightly toward the steering wheel before it would go all the way down to reverse.

Hot wheels — The author and wife, Rita, in Washington, D.C., with their 1952 Oldsmobile 98 Holiday coupe in fall of 1954.

The position was the same as for low gear on the standard, three-speed transmissions with column-mounted shift lever.

Shortly after I bought the car, I rolled absentmindedly to a stop at an intersection. As I waited for the light, I pulled the shift lever toward me and let it drop into the notch just as I would have shifted my previous vehicle into low. When the light changed, I pressed the accelerator and backed rapidly away from the intersection. Fortunately, there was no one behind me!

TODD SHIFTS FOR HIMSELF

The shifting levers of early automatic transmissions had another potential for problems. They were not interlocked with the ignition switch, and they could be moved even if the key was not in the ignition.

Our next-to-youngest son, Todd, displayed an early interest in cars. He could recognize a '57 Plymouth by its tailfins before he was two years old. Tethered to his safety harness between me and Rita in the front seat, he would note the rear fenders of a passing car, try to wrench my head around to follow it, and enthusiastically scream into my right ear, "Plymie, Daddy, Plymie!"

When he was coming up on his second birthday, we were visiting Rita's sister in Iowa City. The house, in the middle of the block, has a steep driveway, and the house across the street stands on a relatively level lot. One day Rita was preparing to go somewhere with at least two of our (then) four children. She placed Todd in a car seat hanging over the back of the front seat, seated daughter Gail on the passenger side, and instructed her to watch him while she went back into the house for something.

Todd reached for the shifting lever; and before Gail could stop him, he pulled it out of the park position. The car rolled down the driveway, across the street, and over the small ash tree that had been planted beside the walk. Hitting the tree caused the car to veer slightly away from the house, and it came to rest in the yard.

Gail was frightened but unhurt. Todd thought the whole business was great fun and couldn't understand what all the fuss was about. Rita was in near panic as she and brother-in-law Kenneth retrieved the car from the neighbor's lawn.

There was no damage to the car, but the tree looked hopeless. I offered to pay for the tree, but the owner propped it up and said, "Let's see what it does."

More than 20 years later, the tree shows a two-and-a-half-foot scar on its trunk, but it is straight and taller than its undamaged mate on the other side of the walk.

We may have been slow learners, because a year later we experienced another lesson while living in a duplex apartment in Ohio. We parked the cars at the end of a double driveway that sloped down toward the backyard which ran downhill to a creek that divided the development.

One day, as Rita busied herself in the kitchen and the kids were playing outside, she noted a yellow car roll across the backyard and stop in the creek. With a start she realized it was our car. When she got to it, there was no one inside, but the neighbor said that when the car stopped, the door opened, and a little boy climbed out and ran to the house. It was Todd. He had climbed into the car and shifted the transmission out of park. After that, we remembered the parking brake.

PUSH-BUTTON SHIFT

We owned one car in particular that Rita didn't like. She probably had good reason. It was a '57 Plymouth station wagon I purchased in 1961 for $250. The age and price should tell you something about it.

As a teacher with a summer newspaper job, I needed something to drive to work so that Rita could use the family car. When I saw this late model offered for such a low price, I knew it would need something, but I reasoned I could fix it up and recover my investment at the end of the summer. I wasn't prepared for all it needed.

First it required a good bath. It had been sitting outdoors in an industrial area of Kansas City for some time. The rocker panels were rusted out, but replacements were available from Warshawsky for a few dollars. The front seal on the transmission leaked, and the engine had a miss from either a burned or stuck valve.

A white station wagon with red top, it washed up to look rather good. Replacing the rocker panels was no big deal, even though pop rivets had not yet been invented. Even the transmission seal proved to be less of a problem than I had anticipated. The two-speed turbomatic used by Chrysler in those days was a rather compact unit, easily unbolted; I had soon slipped a new seal around the shaft and put it back in place.

The valve problem became sticky. I thought grinding the valves would solve it, so I isolated it to the right side of the engine, removed the head, and took it to an automotive machine shop. We found that the valve guides were worn so badly we could not center a mandrel to guide the reseating tool. The head was not made with replaceable valve guides, and the machinist's judgment was that the head would not be worth the expense of reaming and inserting bushings in the valve stem holes.

I set out to find a used head in one of the local salvage yards. To my surprise, I could not find a single one that was not cracked around the valve seats. Apparently that had been a generic weakness in the engine, and usable salvage heads had been snapped up as quickly as they became available.

We reamed the hole to the largest oversize valve stem we could buy, and I took the head home. There I carefully ground a new seat and lapped it by hand to seal the offending valve.

Before I was finished, I also had to replace the rear wheel bearings to quiet a grinding sound in the rear end.

The car ran well after that, and I drove it for three summers before we bought a newer station wagon. (I finally sold it to an Iowa salvage yard for $115.) I was never able to adjust the shifting point on the transmission properly, however; if I lengthened the servo rod to the point where it avoided a lurch when shifting from low to high, it would stay in low range far too long before shifting up.

One other transmission problem could not be blamed on the car. Instead of a shifting lever, the car had a push-button panel on the left side of the dash to select the gears. One bright summer day we went picnicking at the local lake. We parked on a grassy overlook at the edge of a cliff that dropped sharply to the lake. While the rest of us admired the view, my two-year-old son, Scott, busied himself with the knobs and buttons on the dash. I didn't realize what he had been doing until I started the engine to leave. When I reached to push the reverse button on the shifting panel, I discovered he had pushed all the buttons in so far they remained stuck inside the panel housing. I had no tools with me, we were pointed straight at the edge of a cliff, and the transmission was locked in forward gear!

I borrowed a hairpin from Grandma Halsch and probed the buttons. Eventually one yielded, and I was able to coax it back into its proper position. With one unlocked, the others were also freed up, and we were able to drive off without having to call a tow truck. I suppose that was Rita's final reason not to like this car.

OVERHEATED ENGINE

It had been a good day. It was late Sunday afternoon and we were

A pair of cruisers — The family car and boat, affectionately named the "Perry Boat," at the curb in Iowa City in 1959.

returning from a day on the lake. Our '57 Olds Holiday Sedan rolled smoothly along the new highway that had been constructed along the Tuttle Creek Reservoir (once the route of U.S. 77 between Manhattan, Kansas, and Beatrice, Nebraska, along the Big Blue River).

The Olds was a superb car. It had room for our family of six and plenty of trunk space for luggage and picnic gear, and it towed our 16-foot outboard runabout as if it were not there.

About three miles north of town, the road left the lake basin and crossed the last range of the Flint Hills that bordered Manhattan on the north. As we neared the top of the grade, I heard the engine begin to ping. I eased off on the accelerator and looked at the instrument panel. To my surprise, I saw the temperature indicator in the red. I considered pulling over, but since we were almost to the crest of the ridge, I proceeded at a speed that did not cause pinging, expecting the engine to cool on the downgrade on the other side.

It didn't. As we reached the flat four-lane stretch leading into town, the temperature gauge was still in the red. There was a filling station on the opposite side of the road. Attempting to turn into it, I tried to keep the engine running as I waited in the cross-over for oncoming traffic to clear, but it stalled. I attempted to start it again.

To my dismay, it would barely crank. The engine was so hot it was at the point of seizing. I was afraid it would seize if I left it until it cooled, so I cranked it at intervals during the next 45 minutes while the family became increasingly concerned as darkness crept up over the Flint hills.

When the battery ran down, I switched it with the one for the outboard in the boat and continued to crank intermittently. After nearly an hour, I coaxed some life from the engine and eased across the highway to refill the radiator. The engine sounded awfully rough. With the radiator filled, we limped home.

The next day I took the car to the local garage for whatever repairs might be necessary. I wouldn't have given a nickel for the engine's chances of surviving. To my surprise, the service manager reported that the only damage was to the spark plugs, which were burned up. Radiator, valves, and bearings were okay. Compression and oil pressure were normal. The engine ran smoothly again. While I mentally chastised myself for letting the coolant run low, I thanked my good fortune that the car had not been ruined.

I think there was a delayed effect, however. The following summer the car developed a suspicious miss when first started, and after one thousand-mile, trailer-pulling trip, I took it in for a tune-up. Both heads had developed cracks. I didn't know whether to blame the overheating or not. We replaced the heads with one new one the dealer had in stock and another from the salvage yard.

The car again ran like new, and I am still unable to assess whether the cracked head was caused by the overheating or if heads were a weak point in that engine. We drove the car a couple more years as the primary family vehicle and three more years as a second car before we purchased a Mustang.

Shortly before I got rid of the Olds, I had to replace another head. I did this one myself, installing a head salvaged from a junkyard. I figured it was good enough for a nine-year-old car with nearly 100,000 miles on the odometer.

I was saddened to see it a couple of years later, huffing around a mall parking lot with a snow-tread tire on one front wheel, a broken exhaust clearly revealing only seven cylinders firing, and rust eating away its rocker panels and fenders.

LOOSE AXLE

My '61 Olds was running up 80,000 miles. It was performing well, but when I turned a corner to the right, I heard a thump, like a wheel was shifting on the axle.

I left the car for service with a service station mechanic I had come to rely on and asked him to check the rear axle. When I picked it up, he explained that the bearing on the axle had loosened, allowing the axle to shift in and out in response to side pressure on turns.

"It was nothing to fix," he said. "I peened the axle with a center punch before I drove the bearing back in place."

I recognized the old machinist's trick of expanding a shaft to fit a slightly large collar by making indentations with a center punch. The fix is usually temporary, however, and is seldom equal to a press fit.

Puzzled, I inquired what held the bearing on the axle (and thus held the axle in place), since the bearing was positioned in a recess in the axle housing, with a plate secured with bolts around the rim.

I thought he had simply failed to understand the mechanics of the assembly when he said, "Nothing. The bearing is just pressed on the axle."

I hadn't seen the inside of a rear axle assembly since a '50 model, and then there had been a locking ring on the end of the axle shaft inside the differential; it was necessary to remove the banjo cover from the differential and take out the locking device in order to remove the axle shaft.

I knew about the modern tendency to engineer everything for less expensive production, but I couldn't believe a press fit was all that held millions of axles in place.

The tendency for the Oldsmobile's axle to thump on curves was gone, however, so I breathed a little easier as we packed for our summer vacation. Not so easy, however, that I did not supplement my usual kit of wrenches and screwdrivers with some heavy pliers and a machinist's hammer. If that axle came out again, I was going to be prepared to knock it back in place.

With a 16-foot boat in tow and five kids in the back, my wife and I headed out for a month of travel that would take us to visit two sets of grandparents and various friends and relatives throughout the Midwest.

Across Ohio and Michigan, into Minnesota and South Dakota, I checked the axle regularly and found it was staying in proper position. Then as I was negotiating an on-ramp in the interchange from I-35 to I-80 near Des Moines, the car suddenly lost power. I knew immediately what the trouble was. I climbed out and, sure enough, the left rear wheel was as far out from under the car as it could get without tearing off the fender.

While I spoke a few well-chosen words about a suitable place for losing a wheel, Mother said a prayer of thanks that it had not come off while we were wheeling down the Interstate at 60 or 70 miles an hour.

I jacked it up, took off the wheel, removed the bearing plate bolts holding the axle shaft in the housing, and withdrew the axle. The bearing had slipped between two and three inches, enough to let the axle fall out of the spline in the differential. I battered a few more burrs into the shaft to swell its diameter and then hammered the bearing back in place.

In less than 15 minutes, I had the wheel back on and we were again on our way to Grandma's in Iowa City.

Back in Iowa City, I consulted a long-time friend who was the service manager at the Oldsmobile dealership. He assured me that the bearings just snugged on the axle shafts, but it was not quite that simple. Installation required shrinking the shaft by chilling it with dry ice before the bearing was pressed on, so the fit would be super tight. There was no correcting the one that had begun to slip.

I asked him for a replacement axle. He fixed me up with one salvaged from a wrecked car. It lasted as long as I owned the Olds.

MUSTANG MADNESS

INTRODUCING THE PONY CAR

I experienced some difficult moments during Ford Motor Company's introduction of the popular Mustang pony car.

In April 1964, I was in my first year as Director of the School of Journalism at Kent State University. My responsibilities included chairing the student publications policy committee, the nominal governing body for the campus newspaper.

I had spent two quarters with the staff, weeding out the revolutionaries (who wanted to employ the paper for anti-war propaganda) and insulating the editorial positions from the student politicians (who wanted to use the paper for self-promotion). Then along came Ford with a proposition that created a nationwide controversy for campus journalism and set in motion a critical examination of the practices of professional journalism as well.

Ford invited the editors of campus newspapers at 44 of the nation's colleges and universities to come to Detroit for the unveiling of a revolutionary young people's car. The invitation was accompanied by a flight ticket to Detroit and a promise that editors who attended the introductory party would be provided one of the new cars, which they could drive home and use until the end of the school year. A credit card for gasoline was included.

Professional journalists who had just begun to be sensitive to the appearance of corruption connected with favors to writers in the press saw this as a cynical attempt to subvert the ethics of the nation's budding journalists. Newspapers and professional journals alike commented that college editors worthy of their professional aspirations should tell Iacocca and crew thanks, but their support for the new car could not be bought (at least not for the use of a new car for a short time, however attractive it might be).

Editors from four schools turned down the invitation and joined the editorial chorus condemning the cynical motives of Ford. Editors from

39 schools swallowed whatever misgivings they had, if any, and boarded planes for Detroit. We compromised.

The young lady who had just been named editor of our paper was on the spot, and I was on the spot. I had written professionally about the importance of journalistic freedom, had condemned the use of freebies to corrupt the local press, and had developed a course in ethics for students and professionals.

The student government convened a meeting to resolve that the editor should not accept the invitation.

"It and the use of the car should go to the student body president instead," they decided.

Our student chapter of Sigma Delta Chi, a professional journalism society, convened a meeting to ponder whether to recommend that the editor accept the invitation or not. We started with the principle that a journalist should never accept favors that might obligate a writer to a cause or a person.

Others argued that since the Mustang was being offered as a young people's car, it would be appropriate for our editor to drive the car and give her judgment of it. We agreed, as long as it could be made clear that her opinion, whatever it might be, was not a repayment to Ford for its favors.

The editor announced in a front page story that she was returning the free airline tickets and the gasoline credit card, but since there was interest in the car, she would go to the party and drive it home at the expense of the newspaper. She would buy the gasoline for whatever other use the car was put to before it was returned to Ford at the end of the spring term.

To this I added that the car would be turned in to the local dealer according to instructions from Ford and that I would caution that no one connected with the School of Journalism—faculty or student—should expect to purchase the car at a discount.

The editor brought the car back to the campus where it caused a sensation, as Ford assumed it would. It was a caramel-colored convertible with a white top and shift lever on the floor; I recall the attention it attracted when she drove it to the journalism awards dinner. After graduation she turned it in to the local dealer, and I never saw it again.

Our careful efforts to protect our integrity were to no avail. In the storm of criticism that swept through the national press and professional journals, we were lumped with the schools that had accepted the freebies.

No one noticed that we had gone to considerable expense to keep ourselves clean. I guess there was a lesson in more than ethics in the incident.

It didn't sour me on the Mustang, however. I purchased one in the fall of 1966. We drove it until it was rear-ended and totaled one morning in 1982 as I was on my way to work. Pieces of it still serve in the reassembled red fastback I drive today.

LET'S MAKE A DEAL

By mid-summer of 1966 we had decided to purchase a Mustang. In the summer of 1961 I had purchased a worn out Plymouth station wagon to drive back and forth to work to my summer newspaper job.

Rita did not love the car. It had required considerable work, and she had resented the time I devoted to making it serviceable. At the end of summer, we parked it in a shed at Grandma Halsch's place and left it there until we needed it again the following year.

Ride a yellow pony — A yellow Mustang coupe joined the Perry family in 1966.

How about a red fastback? — The author and the red fastback Mustang he prizes today. Many parts from the original yellow coupe still serve in the red fastback, which the author restored for daily driving.

Driver ed class — All five of the Perry children and a couple of neighbor kids learned to drive and qualified for their licenses with the Perrys' 1966 Mustang. Shown with the car are: (from left) Chris, Rita, Todd, and Gail Perry.

During the third summer we realized we had become a two-car family. We decided that with four children, the primary vehicle should be a station wagon, and we would make do with a less expensive second car. By mid-summer, I bought a nearly new Olds station wagon, sold the weary Plymouth to a salvage yard, and relegated the '57 Olds 98 hardtop sedan (that had been the family car) to second car status.

By the summer of 1966, rust was showing through its fenders. Its tires were worn smooth, and I'd had to replace a cracked head with a salvage yard item of questionable vintage. Although I no longer had much of an investment in it, it was expensive to drive around town on errands.

Rita had become enamored of the Mustang. One of her old classmates had become sales manager for the Ford dealer in her hometown, where my brother-in-law, as one of the best customers of the dealership, was regularly given very favorable deals. Since our finances had improved somewhat, and we had planned to visit the hometown, we contacted Rita's classmate to see if we could get a deal on a Mustang.

My commitments made it necessary for Rita and the kids to proceed to Grandma's a week before I could get away; and during the week, with the help of my brother-in-law, she had gone shopping for a Mustang.

By the time I arrived she had picked out two, one red and one yellow. The yellow one, equipped with V8 engine and automatic transmission, suited our purposes. With information from *Consumer Reports*, price lists, and advice from a friend who had formerly owned a new car dealership, I determined I should buy the car for $2,400, about $300 less than the "great deal" price Rita's classmate had quoted her.

When I had driven the car, I told the salesman: "I'll give you $2,400 for it and drive it home."

"You will, like hell!" was his response.

I replied, "I'm leaving Saturday at noon."

At 11:30 on Saturday he phoned and said, "Your car's ready, but you'll have to license it in Iowa in order to get the title. We can get the paperwork done before the courthouse closes if you say the word."

At twelve o'clock, I wrote him a check for $2,445, which included license, tax, and title fees, and we drove the car away.

We drove it back to Ohio the following day, and on the way home I discovered that a fitting on the transmission oil cooler line to the radiator had been cross threaded. I took it to the local dealer for repair. It was the only repair the car needed in the next four years and more than 60,000 miles of driving.

The car remained a member of the family for more than 15 years. All five of our children and at least two of the neighbor kids used it to learn to drive and to qualify for their licenses.

We patched it up with Bondo once, systematically restored it once, and reluctantly gave it up only after a collision in which it was rear-ended by a high school student driving a Jeep. It was reduced to a pile of rusted tin, but even that was not the end. The power train and miscellaneous interior parts were transferred to a replacement vehicle I assembled, and some of it remains in service in the red '66 fastback I drive today.

Recently, when I was installing a later model engine in the '66, one of my friends was admiring the sleek lines of the fastback in awe.

"How long you had this baby?" he inquired.

"That's hard to say," I replied, "In various incarnations, about 26 years."

Indeed, the yellow '66 hardtop coupe had undergone an engine transplant sometime in the '70s, when a leaking head gasket had destroyed the engine. With that engine and some body restoration, it saw my eldest son through college, and when he was able to purchase a fastback of his own, he returned it to me. I drove it to work regularly, until that frosty January morning when the high school student in the out-of-control jeep hit it in the rear end.

With the insurance settlement from that, I bought the red fastback that had lived its life in a climate unafflicted with salted streets, and I transferred the power train and interior to this second body. After it saw my youngest son through college and I got it back again, I did a thorough restoration, intending to drive it for an long time. By the time my friend made his inquiry, only the steering wheel, the rear axle, and the seat frames of the original car were left, so his question was hard to answer.

TOO MANY GASKETS

The Mustang was fairly new. It was nearing the time for an oil change, and I was planning some travel, so (in a variation from my usual practice of doing my own maintenance) I dropped it off at a neighborhood service station and picked it up on my way out of town.

That afternoon, as I was breezing along the expressway east of Cleveland, I began to hear a lot of valve clatter, which I associated with a battered Chevy that appeared in my rearview mirror. When the Chevy peeled off into a far left lane, I realized that the noise was coming from my own car. I dropped my eyes to the instrument panel and, to my horror, saw the oil gauge flicker from zero to mid-range, then drop again to zero.

As I was approaching an off-ramp, I shut the engine down and coasted to the stop sign at the end of the ramp. There was a service station about a block to my right, so I went for aid.

When the station attendant lifted the hood, we found the left side of the engine compartment bathed in oil. We checked the oil level. Nothing showed on the dipstick. We added a couple of quarts to bring it up to a level we could see, then drove the car onto the hoist. It left a two-foot-wide trail of oil from where it stood all the way into the service bay, throwing out most of the oil we had just poured in.

It didn't take long to diagnose the trouble. When the attendant had changed the oil filter that morning, the gasket from the old filter had stuck to the engine block. The new filter had been installed with its gasket on top of the old. Since the seal was not confined to the recess in the base of the filter, it lasted less than a hundred miles before it blew out.

At that point, I wouldn't have given a nickel for the engine's prospects. We replaced the failed gasket, filled the crankcase with oil, and added a quart of STP for good measure. I drove home.

Although the engine performed as usual, I was far from reassured. I confronted the operator of the station where the car had been serviced. He was obviously apprehensive as he faced the loss of a customer and the prospect that he might have to replace my engine. He promised a free change of oil and asked me to continue driving the car until we could determine how much harm had been done.

To my surprise (and to his great relief), the engine continued to be healthy. It ran nearly 70,000 miles before it was done in by a leaking head gasket, a problem obviously not related to lubrication.

A JOB FOR EXPERTS

One day while I was changing the oil in the faithful Mustang, I poked a rusty spot on the side of the left torque box frame with a screwdriver and, to my dismay, discovered that the metal was completely rusted away. A hole nearly three inches in diameter appeared when I flaked away the rust.

I had been fighting rust on the car for five years (it was now ten years old). I had replaced the engine and brazed patches on the fenders when I found that the fiberglass rust repairs were good for only a couple of years, at best. It still looked good and drove well, and we wanted to keep it, but I knew the frame would have to be repaired. The small brazing torch I had used to patch the fenders hardly seemed equal to the task of welding a new vertical section into the frame member. And besides, I would need a piece of vanadium or other high-strength steel to make the repair.

In the classified section of our local newspaper, I found an answer to my dilemma.

''Frames Repaired,'' the ad said. ''Specialists in all kinds of frame welding and straightening.''

I took the car to the shop, which was located in a nearby small town. I explained to the young workman (who appeared to understand that I felt that the upper and lower elements of the section were sound) how he could cut a piece to duplicate the web section of the rusted part's H configuration and arc weld it in place. He said his boss knew exactly how to fix it, so I left the car.

When I returned, I found they had cut a C section piece from a heavy frame of a junked vehicle, wrapped it around the torque box of the Mustang, and welded it in place. It looked clumsy and patched up, but the boss assured me it would be as strong as new. He pointed out that it had been necessary to splice the brake line where it crossed the frame, because the line was in the way of the repair and wouldn't reach all the way to its mounting after going around the new member. He pointed to a new brass coupling where the brake line passed from inside to outside the frame.

With some dismay, I paid his forty-some-dollar bill and drove the car home. At the first right turn I encountered, I almost ditched the car. Although I turned the wheel all the way to lock, I couldn't negotiate the turn. When I looked under the car, I discovered the bunglesome patch interfered with the steering arm and prevented the car from making a full turn.

I immediately drove back to the shop. The welder crawled under the car with a cutting torch and hacked away until his assistant could turn the wheel all the way and then told me:

''It'll be alright now. Didn't weaken her a bit.'' I drove home again, not much comforted that I could now steer the car.

The following day, one of my teenage sons drove the car away shortly before I set out behind him in another vehicle. At the stop sign two blocks from the house, he drove right through and then turned into a driveway in the middle of the block. Sensing trouble, I pulled up behind him and stopped. He was obviously frightened.

"I don't have any brakes," he said.

I tried the pedal. It went to the floor. Under the left front wheel I saw fluid dripping.

"Step on them again," I said as I peered under the car.

As he applied pressure to the pedal, brake fluid squirted from the brass coupling the mechanic had installed. One end of the spliced line had pulled out of the coupling.

We inched the car back to my garage, where I took the coupling apart to see if the flare had been crimped too tightly and had broken off. There was no flare! The frame expert had spliced the brake line using press-on copper ferules suitable for a fuel line connection!

I replaced the spliced brake line with a new one from the auto parts store, but for the rest of its life the Mustang bore scars of butchery from the "frame expert."

CAPRI CAPERS

OL' SMOKEY

By the fall of 1974 Rita and I had decided that it was time to replace the '66 Mustang. The ideal replacement seemed to be a new Mercury Capri, a sporty little car, which (although smaller than the Mustang) was fitted with nearly identical bucket and bench seats for four people.

I visited with the local Mercury dealer. He had three or four of the cars in stock. Prices ranged between $2,700 and $2,900. The salesman pressured me to buy one with the standard sales pitch: "You'd better buy one of these '74s, because the prices are going up $400 next year!"

My natural disposition is to resist such sales tactics, and the pitch turned me off. Besides, I felt I could buy one at the end of the model

Mustang replacement — Murv and Rita Perry and their 1974 Capri photographed in Iowa City about 1980.

year at a discount. I responded predictably and walked out of the showroom.

The following spring we went shopping for a '75 model. To our dismay, we discovered the salesman had been right! He was more than right. The deluxe coupe we picked out with air, stereo, and V6 engine was now priced at $5,500. It was beyond our price range and we abandoned our intention to replace the Mustang that year.

The next year, with new car prices still rising and the Mustang rusting rapidly from eight years in the salted streets of northeastern Ohio, we went shopping for a good used Capri. The first one we looked at was offered by a private owner who had moved up to a Datsun 240Z. It was a pretty red coupe with a four-speed transmission and a V6 engine. It ran well, but it had more than 60,000 miles on the odometer, and it had a ticking tappet that disturbed me. I didn't know at the time that the tappets were mechanically adjustable, and envisioned hydraulic lifters and an expensive replacement problem.

The price was also a concern. Even though the car was two years old and had high mileage, the owner wanted $3,000. Feeling the price might be negotiable, I took the car home to show Rita. We took it for a drive, which was probably a mistake. She loved the look of it, but when I turned the wheel over to her she had trouble with the clutch and stalled at a difficult intersection. When we got back home, she said, "You can buy it, but I won't drive it."

I took it back and continued looking. A month or so later, I discovered a beige Capri ("Desert Sand" was the official color) on a dealer's lot. The paint and upholstery were flawless, and it had a dark brown vinyl top that gave it just the sporty look we wanted. The odometer reading was quite low for a two-year-old car, but the previous owner testified to its accuracy in a phone conversation, insisting that the car had never been in the shop for either body or mechanical work. He lied, but that's another story.

Swallowing some misgivings about a slightly noisy exhaust and the greater vibrations attributed to the four-cylinder engine, we bought it, resentfully conscious that we were paying $3,200 for a two-year-old used car that we could have purchased new for $2,800.

As I drove the Capri (although I was satisfied with the look and feel of the car on the road), I was uneasy about two things: a vibration I noticed at city traffic speeds and a somewhat loud exhaust.

I attributed the exhaust noise to a loose connection at the point where the tailpipe attached to the muffler, but when I attempted to tighten it, I found that the clamp didn't fit. That wasn't all. When I bought a new, properly-sized clamp, I found that the pipe and the muffler were not matched. One was sized in inches and the other was metric. It took some shimming and bushing to quiet the exhaust.

There was still the vibration. The car shook at city traffic speeds so that images of following vehicles in the rearview mirror were undistinguishable. I assumed this was the nature of the four-cylinder beast, and mourned the V8 Mustang.

Before the end of the summer, I noticed smoke coming from the exhaust. I tried to ignore it, but obviously I was conscious of it as I was of every smoking vehicle in traffic. One day in my station wagon, I braked for a traffic light. I noticed a considerable amount of smoke drifting among cars waiting for the light at the cross street. As the light changed and the cars moved across in front of me, I saw that the smoke seemed to come primarily from one beige-colored coupe. As it disappeared in a cloud of blue smoke, I realized it was my car!

Although the odometer still showed only 50,000 miles, I decided it was time for an overhaul. I removed the engine and disassembled it. Three pistons bore the markings of the factory. The fourth was different. I had discovered the source of the vibration. I did a little judicious grinding and balancing before I reassembled the engine. Crank journals and cylinder wall dimensions were all within stock tolerances, so I concluded that the smoking was caused by cooked valve stem seals.

I had the valves ground, honed the cylinders, and put the engine back together with new rings and bearing inserts. With another valve job somewhere beyond 100,000 miles, it purred on for 140,000 miles over the next ten years, until the son to whom it had been handed down traded it for a new Mercury Lynx.

TWO MORE CAPRIS

After the overhaul cured the smoke and vibration problems with the Capri, we were so pleased with it that we purchased two additional coupes for the kids to drive.

I first saw the second one on a dealer's lot with only the driver's side exposed to view and a relatively low price displayed. When I stopped to inspect it, I found both right fenders had been damaged in a sideswipe accident. I was about to leave when the salesman asked, "What would you give for that car?"

With little thought, I divided his asking price in half and said, "I'll give you $400 if it runs."

He started it up but kept the engine racing.

"It has a choke problem," he said above the roar. "The idle is set too high."

I wrote him a check, drove it home, and hid it in the garage. Then I set about repairing the bent fenders with a big hammer and a large can of Bondo.

When I had restored the appearance sufficiently to move it out of the garage, I tackled the carburetor. I discovered one of the idle jets was missing. With it replaced, I adjusted things until the engine idled satisfactorily and didn't stall in traffic. Then I discovered the reason for the messed-up carburetor.

The noise of the high revving engine effectively covered up the sound of seriously loose connecting rod bearings. It was time for another overhaul.

To my surprise, I found that despite the clatter of an obviously worn-out bearing, none of the crank journals were out of round, and the cylinder walls showed practically no taper. With the help of an automotive machinist who ground the valves, I reassembled the car and gave it to my second son to drive to school and to work. He racked up more than 100,000 miles during the next eight years before he finished college and then got a full-time job and traded it for a new Chevy Blazer.

CARBURETORS

I learned about carburetors mostly by trial and error (mostly trial and one hell of a lot of error). After I rebuilt the carburetor on the Capri, my son was driving to work, and he complained that it was getting terrible gas mileage. I checked carefully, and after finding that it was properly assembled and set (as far as I could tell), I sent him back on the road while I pondered the possible cause.

There seemed to be little reason that a small four-cylinder car was getting only 12 miles to the gallon. I read the service manual carefully and took the carburetor apart again. As I was about to replace the brass jets in the bottom of the carburetor bowl, I noticed a small number stamped on one of them. I compared it to the other and found they were different. I examined the jets carefully.

One had a larger hole in the center. Aha! I had the solution. When

I had earlier cleaned the carburetor, I had reversed the jets, installing the larger high-speed jet in the primary barrel of the carburetor and the smaller in the secondary barrel.

With the jets properly installed, the Capri again delivered its customary 22-26 miles per gallon.

There was one carburetor trick on the Capri, however, that I never did figure out. When I went to service the carburetor on one of the three we owned, I found that the idle jet on one side of the carburetor had been replaced with a grease fitting. At that time I had owned the car for more than five years and had experienced no idle or performance problems. When I replaced the jet, I found I had trouble setting the idle satisfactorily, so I put the grease fitting back in, and the car ran until we traded it.

CAPRI TROUBLES

The third Capri we purchased gave me fits a couple of times. I induced my daughter to buy it to drive to her first job as a nurse in the local hospital. She was just out of college and had not accumulated enough money for the down payment on an expensive car, and since I was changing jobs and moving to a distant state, the fleet of family cars would no longer be available to her.

We found a beige coupe just like the one her mother drove except for the four-speed transmission and vinyl top. The price was within range of her budget, and the car seemed to be in good shape.

When we got it home, I noticed a problem. The switch lock was worn. Sometimes it was necessary to jiggle the key before the switch would turn. I thought perhaps a little oil or graphite in the lock would cure it. I was wrong. The second day we had it, Gail found she could not turn the key to get it started. I couldn't either. I set about to repair it.

Rather than destroy the lock trying to get it out of its housing on the steering column, I went to the parts department of the local Mercury garage. The young attendant there and I had developed a pretty good relationship. (It began when I bought a heater control valve for which he charged me $19.00. In jest, I had said, "The same part for a Pinto is only $13.00." He quickly denied it, but the next time I came in for parts, he took me aside and said, "I looked that part up after you left, and you were right. The same part for the Pinto lists at $13.00 and carries the same part number.")

For the lock, he had a replacement lock cylinder, but the problem remained to get the old cylinder out. He told me the shop procedure called for drilling a one-eighth inch hole at a precise spot on the underside of the housing and pushing a small screwdriver or nail into the hole to release a detent spring that held the lock in place.

I was lucky, because I hit the place exactly with the first hole I drilled and was able to install the new switch in less than half an hour.

Unfortunately, I forgot to note the location of where to drill the hole, and a couple of years later, when it became necessary to replace the switch on one of the other Capris, I wound up drilling a succession of holes before I found the right spot.

Another problem didn't seem so big at the outset. There was a short in the electrical system. It showed up a day or so before I left town, blowing a fuse when I turned on the windshield wiper. I checked the circuits, replaced the fuse, and hoped for the best.

The best didn't happen. The car repeatedly blew fuses. My son, who had remained behind to attend the local college, traced the circuits, wire by wire. We conferred by phone as we pored over the wiring diagrams to try to determine where there could be a short that would blow a fuse under the circumstances. The problem seemed to get worse after a rain, which caused us to suspect the windshield wiper and to look for any place where moisture could enter and cause a short circuit.

He finally found it in a frozen back-up light switch.

MORE PROBLEMS

Two other problems with that car gave me a bad time. After a particularly hard drive, Gail found that the car overheated and stalled. A neighbor who had helped her get it started found that it had run out of oil. She had nursed it down to Tennessee for a visit and, although the engine didn't sound unhealthy, I decided it should be opened up for an overhaul since it had been using a considerable amount of oil.

When I opened the engine, I found how close she had come to destroying it. The babbitt in the front connecting rod bearing insert had become hot enough to run. A fleck the width of a toothpick had adhered to the crankshaft and had scored the insert. However, I was able to dislodge the fleck and polish the journal, which had not been damaged.

In short order, I had the valves done, installed new rings and inserts, and had the car ready to be put back on the road. Unhappily, I found that it smoked. I decided I should drive it a while until the rings seated, and sent her back to work with one of my cars.

Instead of abating, the smoking got worse. I considered the possible causes. Rings? They were new! With the oil filler cap off, I could feel a vacuum on the crankcase. Replace the PCV valve? I did so, but to no avail.

Nothing helped. I thought of the valve stem seals, but surely they were good. The valves had been done by a machinist at the local auto parts store.

I pulled the valve cover. (I didn't like doing this, because it almost always requires replacing an expensive gasket; and even with a new gasket, getting that valve cover to seal without a leak is a pain.) It didn't take long to discover the trouble. The seals were riding up and down on the valve stems. They had not been buttoned down over the ends of the valve guides.

Faced with the twin prospects of having to pull the head and pay for new gaskets, I complained to the parts shop that had done the work. They were embarrassed. They had hired a young trainee from the local vocational school on the recommendation of a teacher who had a long association with the shop. They would make it right. If I would give them time to confer with the teacher, they would let me know what they could do.

The teacher was embarrassed, too. He had thought the young mechanic was better prepared than he had been. He asked me to bring the car to the school shop on Saturday afternoon. Working quickly, he pulled the valve cover from the head, removed the spark plug from the first cylinder, and screwed in a compressed air adapter. With the cylinder on the compression stroke, he filled the chamber with compressed air to hold the valves in place, removed the valve springs, and seated the offending seals. When he had replaced the springs and keepers, he repeated the procedure with each of the other three cylinders in turn.

The job required less than an hour, and when he was finished, the smoking ceased. I sent the car back to Gail in Ohio for another year of service before she traded it in.

THE RED BUTTON

There was another electrical quirk that I was never able to understand. The '74 Capri models had come with an interlock between the seat belt and the starting system. The controller for the system was located behind the kick panel in the left side of the rear seat. There was a red emergency button mounted on the firewall under the hood that would set the starter to be activated one time if the seat belts were not buckled. This was (apparently) to allow a mechanic to start the car from under the hood if no one was buckled into the driver's seat.

Before we acquired the car, someone had disconnected the interlock or otherwise made it inoperative, except when the weather was very cold. In low temperatures, the controller apparently assumed that the seat belts were not buckled and deactivated the starter. You could get one start by raising the hood, pressing the red reset button, and getting back in the driver's seat to start the car. If the engine stalled (as it was wont to do when it was cold), the driver had to get out, raise the hood, and press the little red button again.

Working a night shift at the hospital, Gail spent a miserable couple of months before she was able to bring the car home so I could remove the interlock system.

MISSED DIAGNOSIS

Gail had made up her mind to trade the Capri for a new Buick Regal or an Oldsmobile Cutlass, whichever she could get the best deal on. She had been working for more than two years and had the down payment and monthly installments for a new car.

Her decision was hastened by trouble with the Capri. It was running poorly. She had taken it to a local service station where the mechanic found the front spark plug fouled and the cylinder filled with oil. He advised her that she probably had a broken piston.

In attempting to arrange a trade, she found she could get a better deal buying a Buick outright than she could get trading the old car in. She bought the Buick and left the Capri sitting in the garage until I came to help her dispose of it.

When I had a couple of days off, I packed a pair of coveralls, loaded up a toolbox, and accompanied her home. The next morning I pulled the spark plugs and, sure enough, the front cylinder was filled with oil. Since I had confidence in the service station operator who had advised Gail, the broken piston diagnosis sounded reasonable. I pulled the head. The cylinder was full of oil, but there was no evidence of a broken piston from the top of the motor.

Maybe it was a broken ring. I unbuttoned the crankcase and popped all four pistons out of the cylinders. I found nothing wrong. Vexed,

I replaced the pistons, oil pan, and head and started the engine. Since I had cleaned the oil from the cylinder and spark plug, it ran beautifully, although there was a little smoke.

With the engine running, I began to adjust the idle (which the mechanic at the service station had set a little high to prevent stalling when the engine was running on only three cylinders). Not only could I not get it set right, the more I adjusted it, the worse it ran. At last it began missing and smoking and acting just like it had a blown piston.

I pulled the PCV valve from its housing and turned it upside down to inspect it. There was no valve in the casing.

When I had put things back together, I had noticed a washer lying in the bottom of the box that attached the PCV valve to the manifold, and wondered how it had been dropped in there. I never thought to inspect the valve carefully, since I had replaced it the last time I had changed the oil. It was the problem, though. What we had thought was a broken piston turned out to be a defective PCV valve that had spilled its guts into the manifold, allowing the engine to suck oil directly into the cylinders. I was embarrassed that I had disassembled the engine before discovering it.

I replaced the valve, sold the Capri to a friend who had been waiting to buy it for his kids to drive, put my toolbox under my arm, and took the bus home.

THE ALL-PURPOSE AUTOMOBILE

PUMPING WATER

I learned about ignition from the one-cylinder gasoline engine we used to pump water for the cows when I was a boy. Our rented farm had about 35 acres of pasture, enough for the small herd of cattle (two cows and seven heifers) and six draft animals (four horses and two mules). There was no well, but water was really not a problem, since the lower acres of the pasture lay on Sioux River bottomland. A person could dig a hole with a post auger, drive a four-foot sandpoint, and have a well.

Pumping was a problem. In those days, windmills marked the farmsteads, providing water for livestock. On the up-to-date farms, running water was supplied to the house as well.

Windmills, however, cost hundreds of dollars, and they were considered permanent, which meant that once installed they could not be moved off the property by the renter (becoming, effectively, the property of the land's owner). Our landlord was not about to erect a windmill on those bare acres, so if we wanted water, we would have to pump it.

Dad dug a well and installed a pump, and at nine and ten years of age, my brother and I were given the daily task of pumping water. It was hard work, and hardest on hot days when the animals drank the most.

We knew of a device called a "Helping Henry," which fitted rollers under the rear wheels of a Model T to drive a pulley to supply power for farm chores. Dad found a way to make the chore easier using only part of the family car. He bought a pump jack for $.50 and an engine for $1.50, except the engine didn't run. It didn't run because a key part of the ignition system (something called an "igniter") was missing. What's more, although the engine bore the name "John Deere," the relationship to the implement manufacturer was so cloudy that the local dealer could not obtain a replacement for the spark device.

Pumping water was a chore — Earl Perry is shown at the farm pump in the early 1920s.

Examination of other engines revealed that the "igniter" was a combination spark plug and timer that was tripped by the valve mechanism to fire the fuel when the valves were closed.

Dad found that a spark plug from the Model T would screw into the threaded hole in the cylinder head where the missing "igniter" was supposed to fit. With it in place, he improvised other parts for an ignition system using a hacksaw blade, the battery, and one of the four vibrator coils from the Model T.

The hacksaw blade served as the timer. He positioned it so that when the cylinder was to fire, a small protrusion on the cam came into contact with the blade, completing a circuit through the primary winding of the coil. This set the vibrator coil to singing, inducing a high voltage current in the secondary winding, which was connected to the spark plug. The engine fired.

A centrifugal weight attached by a spring to the flywheel would move outward as the engine increased its speed and, at maximum revolutions, strike a ratchet lever that would lock the exhaust valve open until speed decreased. This gave the engine a distinctive sound. It would fire with a puffing pop two or three times, then coast for several revolutions with a huffing sound. Then it would fire again, once or twice, before going into the coasting routine.

Jerry-built or not, the homemade ignition worked. The engine pumped for three or four years until we moved to a farm with a windmill. When the battery ran down, it was reinstalled in the T so the generator could recharge it. When it was being used for the pump engine, the T could be run on the magneto. It merely meant we had to crank the T, but that was no big deal, since the starter didn't work much of the time anyway; and cranking the old Ford sure beat hell out of pumping water.

Fifty years later, I applied the same fix to my outboard motor. When the manufacturer said the third replacement ignition module would cost more than $300, I substituted a homemade ignition system. Instead of a hacksaw blade, I used a Jeep ignition module, a Ford coil, and lawn mower spark plugs for a total cost of less than $75. Four years later, even though it has now seen more than 20 years of service, the old outboard will still rev up to 5,500 rpms and pull two water-skiers.

I always keep a roll of baling wire in my toolbox. I learned that from Dad.

Old cars become trailers — Henry Eichel uses a trailer made from a Model T chassis to haul brush that will be chopped up for firewood. Picture taken near Bruce, S.D., in the late 1920s.

OLD AUTOS NEVER DIE, THEY JUST TRAIL AWAY

As early automobiles wore out, they often wound up as trailers on the farms and in the small towns of rural America. As farmers moved to fancier cars, they stripped the bodies and engines from the T chassis and converted the running gears into serviceable utility haulers.

Two- and four-wheel versions were built. The two-wheeled version was most popular for reasons of handling and size. It took a skilled driver to back a four-wheel unit, even when all hitch and steering elements were tight and properly designed (which often they were not). The greater load capacity of four-wheel trailers tended to overload the cars of the day.

Some merely added a tow bar ("tongue" in farm vernacular, adapted from the term for the wagon pole used between the hitch of horses which served to steer the wagon) to the stripped chassis. Often the tongue was linked to the tie rods to employ the auto steering, but since few of the barnyard mechanics understood the geometry of steering, the easy layout of tie rods and drag links resulted in a chronic oversteer on most rigs. This made them unsuitable for towing at highway speeds, as they would weave back and forth behind the tow vehicle and make the rig uncontrollable.

At horse and tractor speeds, the auto steering had an advantage over the conventional wagon steering; even on the sharpest turn the front wheels remained firmly under the corners of the load, instead of retreating toward the center as they did with wagon steering. This created instability that could cause unbalanced loads to tip, but for highway towing, a trailer with a solid front axle and wagon steering would follow a vehicle with greater stability.

Solutions to these problems were as numerous as the mechanics who built trailers, and despite some shortcomings inherent in the original chassis or the trailer builder's design, almost every farm used one or more trailers.

One of the more interesting trailer ideas I encountered involved a pusher trailer built by a Brookings County, S.D., farmer to enable him to travel at road speeds with his older model tractor.

It was not uncommon to equip tractors made in the '30s and early '40s with rubber tires. Many were converted to rubber after suitable tires were developed about 1936, but until the beginning of the '40s, speeds were limited to six or seven miles per hour at the most. Some of the '40s models had "road gears" that would go 12 to 18 miles an hour.

To provide greater speed, the farmer built a trailer using the rear axle of an automobile. Leaving the drive shaft and differential intact, he bolted the transmission to the drive shaft near the hitch. With the trailer hitched to the tractor, he connected the tractor's power take off to the input shaft of the transmission.

When he wanted to go fast, he shifted the tractor into neutral, engaged the power take off, and shifted up through the gears of the trailer transmission behind his seat.

My brother and I liked the idea and tried to adapt it to our purposes. We already had a trailer built from a Model T rear end. We lacked the transmission, but we thought we would try it with Dad's old F12 to see how practical it might be. We found that by slipping the clutch, we could get the rig moving; but when we opened the throttle on the gravel road, we quickly determined we had more than we could handle.

The brakes on the tractor were primitive and were operated by hand levers at either side of the tractor. Two hands were required to stop the machine, leaving none for steering. In addition, the speed attained with the throttle only partially open set the tractor to bouncing furiously on its single balloon-tired front wheel. Within half a mile we decided the transit trailer needed considerably more refinement before we could put it to use.

We resolved to study the gearing and install a transmission to provide an acceptable ratio and speed, but other things got priority, and we both left the farm before the trailer was completed.

PARTS FOR EVERYTHING

Just as a Model T had provided the power and chassis for Grandpa Eichel's mobile disc grinder, discarded automobiles provided a ready source of parts for inventive farmers of the late '30s and '40s as they adapted horse-drawn farm implements for use with tractors.

Perhaps the most ingenious of all was the haystacker which came to be known as a "Jayhawker," the registered name of a machine produced in Kansas and widely copied by build-it-yourself farmers across the Midwest.

Before the days of the twine baler, the chopper, and silo storage of grasses, farmers handled hay the old-fashioned way—with a pitchfork. The hay was mowed, raked into windrows, gathered by hand, and stored in barns or in outdoor stacks as high as a man could throw it with as big a fork as he could handle.

Making hay — A buckrake, or bucker, was used to move hay to the stacks on the Eichel farm near Bruce, S.D., in the early 1920s.

The pitchfork came to be augmented by the buckrake, or "bucker," and the stacker. The bucker was really a large fork, eight to ten feet wide with six-foot tines made of wood. With a horse hitched at each side, the bucker could be guided down a windrow of hay to gather a huge load that could then be dragged across the field to the stack. Here the stacker (a derrick with a similar large wood fork) would receive the hay and lift it to the top of the pile.

When tractors replaced horsepower, the bucker and stacker were combined into an ungainly contraption to be pushed around the hay fields ahead of the tractor to gather the hay and lift it to the stacks in a continuous operation.

As the configuration of the row crop tractor evolved, the "Jayhawker" was mounted directly on the tractor, much like a large contemporary forklift, making it much more convenient to maneuver than the jointed unit that had to be steered around the fields like a trailer in reverse.

When plans for such a hay-making machine were published in a popular farm magazine, many farmers built them with more or less ingenious and workable adaptations of their own.

At the heart of the farm-built unit was the rear axle and differential of a junked auto. Mounted across the rear of the tractor, it provided the mechanics for both the continuously running clutch (to engage the cable hoist that lifted the load) and the brake (to hold it at a manageable level for travel across the field).

With the drive pinion shaft connected to the power take off shaft of the tractor, live power was available at each end of the axle assembly. A drum, mounted where one wheel would have been, wound a cable to lift the load. Levers within easy reach of the operator controlled each wheel brake separately. When both brakes were released, power passed through the differential to the free wheel end of the axle, which spun idly.

When the brake on the free wheel was locked, power was transferred to the winch, winding the cable and lifting the hay. When the brake on the winch hub was locked, the load could be held clear of the ground for travel to the point where it could be further lifted to the stack. A skilled operator soon learned to judge when to engage the lift so that the load reached its peak height just as the rig reached the stack, so the hay could be placed without any loss of motion. Elaborate rigs used a trip device to dump the load like a modern payloader. More primitive ones were unloaded by lowering the load to the top of the stack, then shifting the tractor into reverse and backing away.

Of course, it wasn't long until another inventive farmer substituted a three-foot fork with heavy steel tines and used the same tractor-mounted device to load manure. To work within the confines of barnyards and animal sheds, the dimensions of the derrick were scaled down as the ruggedness of the lift was beefed up, but control of the lifting continued to be provided by axle and differential units scavenged from worn-out family autos.

WHEELS OF PROGRESS

In the mid-1930s, a wholesale shift of farm implements from steel-shod wheels to rubber tires occurred. All three of the major rubber companies had developed tires that would carry a tractor and provide traction necessary to pull a plow. Manufacturers began to supply new implements with pneumatic-tired wheels. Individual farmers and local blacksmiths undertook to convert existing tractor and horse-drawn implements to rubber tires.

Rural blacksmiths welded 16-inch drop-center rims to the cut off spokes of wagon (and other implement) wheels. The 600-16 tire became universal. It was fitted to any implement that moved on wheels. And for those that did not, trucks were designed to lift them from job to job.

For the conversions, tires that had become unserviceable for the family car were often sufficiently usable for fields. A damaged tire could be repaired to carry loads of hay and grain at the speeds of horses or farm tractors.

A most popular conversion for wagons involved discarding most of the wagon running gear, keeping only the bolsters, frame, and axles, which were sawed off at each end. A car axle was then bolted underneath so that the wheels were held in the same position as the original wheels.

Axles and disc wheels from old Chevys worked best. Rims could easily be welded on the cut down discs. Artillery-type wheels with wood spokes were useless, and wire wheels involved centering and welding skills most rural welders did not possess.

The best wagons were made from two front axles. Using the rear axle caused problems with lubrication and strength. I am not surprised to find such wagons in use on smaller farms today. And bigger, newer rigs supplied by the implement makers today follow a similar design, but they are engineered for heavier duty.

THE SNAP IS GONE

Tires have changed. In the '20s, even the most visionary tire makers could scarcely have conceived of the tubeless balloon cushions that our cars roll on today. I recall that one of the two extra spares Dad kept strapped to the bracket meant for holding the top on his Model T roadster had a tread composed of little vacuum cups. These cups were supposed to make it hold the road, and Firestone wasn't bashful about its claims when it molded the letters "Non-Skid" into the tread of its early tires.

I'm equally certain the rubber chemists who substituted butyl for natural rubber and then abandoned inner tubes altogether never realized how they were depriving a generation of growing boys of the power source for some of their most-enjoyed toys: the rubber band shooter and the slingshot.

A one-half inch wide section of inner tube made ideal ammunition for a variety of ingeniously crafted rubber band guns that sometimes looked like the real thing, depending on the skill of the maker. A crude favorite was to cut a block of wood into a pistol shape, fasten a spring clothespin to the handle, clip one end of a rubber band in the jaw of the clothespin, and stretch the other over the barrel end of the gun. When the handle was squeezed, the rubber band would snap in whatever direction the gun was pointed.

The standard slingshot used two strips of rubber one-half inch wide and 12 to 14 inches long. One end of each strip was lashed to the fork ends of a crotch cut from a tree branch. The other ends were fastened to a pouch made from shoe leather, into which a stone could be inserted. Using the third member of the crotch for a handle, the pouch was pulled back, and the strips were stretched to arm's length before being released to hurl the stone with much greater distance and accuracy than it could be thrown.

Some of my young friends were adept at picking sparrows off telephone wires with such a homemade slingshot. I don't know why they wanted to shoot sparrows, since the little green glass insulators on the telephone line made just as good targets; although the telephone man got awfully upset when he caught us breaking them.

PARKING TICKETS

NO MISTAKE

The first parking ticket I received was a complete surprise. Still in the service, but back in the States and just married, I was living with my new wife in an upstairs apartment just off the main drag in East Greenwich, R.I. I bought a pretty little Ford coupe. In the late afternoon, I proudly parked it in front of the house where several other cars stood.

When I had occasion to drive it a day or two later, I noticed what appeared to be a shipping tag tied to the shaft of the windshield wiper. I thought it was an identifying tag the dealer I had bought the car from had failed to remove. As I started down the street, the wind flipped the tag over, and I saw in bold letters, "EAST GREENWICH POLICE DEPARTMENT."

I stopped the car to examine the tag. It was a parking ticket. Melting snow had caused the ink to run, and it was impossible to decipher just what the violation was. My first thought was the ticket had been on the car when I bought it. I proceeded to the police station a few a blocks away to clear up the misunderstanding.

It was not a misunderstanding. When he learned my address, the officer in charge told me the ticket was mine and what it was for. I had failed to note, as I parked among the row of cars in front of the house, that the area was posted to prohibit overnight parking. Although there were other cars parked there when I drove up, I never noticed that they were moved during the evening. I sheepishly paid the $2.50 fine.

Another ticket I got was also a surprise. I wish it could have been as inexpensive.

Rita and I were driving through the area near the Ohio State University campus in Columbus one hot summer afternoon on our way to visit friends in northern Ohio where we had once lived. A Baskin-Robbins ice cream store attracted our attention, and as a car pulled away from the curb directly in front of it, I pulled into the vacated space, noting that the sign on the nearby lamppost said, "No Parking After 4 p.m." I checked my watch. It was a few minutes before four.

The store was busier than we had anticipated, and it was some time before we could get waited on. Just as we were handed our order, a young woman (probably a student at Ohio State) rushed in and shouted, "They're towing cars!" I rushed outside just in time to see my car disappearing around the corner behind a tow truck. I checked my watch. It was one minute after four!

I protested to the officer supervising a second tow being made ready. He radioed the truck, but it was too late; my car was on the way to the city impound lot on the south edge of town.

With directions to the pound, we boarded a bus and after an hour's ride arrived at the gate where the attendant told us we must go back up to city hall to pay the fine and towing charge.

After another bus ride back up town, we learned that the fine and towing charge amounted to $68.00, which we had to pay in cash or put on a credit card. No checks would be accepted. As I grudgingly paid the fine, the clerk admonished me, "Now you'll have to prove ownership before they will release the car to you."

I assured her that would be no problem since the registration certificate was in the car.

"But you can't have access to the car until you prove ownership," she said.

I told her what I thought of that.

It was to no avail. The only recourse was a phone call to the department of motor vehicle registration in Nashville, Tenn., in the hope that there would be some way to verify my ownership of the car even though it was now well past six o'clock in the evening.

That call was my only piece of good luck during the day. A Nashville clerk cheerfully assured the Ohio bureaucrat that I did indeed own the car in question. That individual, with what seemed to me a continued air of defiance, initialed a release order for the pound attendant.

Another bus ride and another very hostile confrontation with the attendant (who didn't know where the car had been parked and who felt he should not have to look for it until the following morning) eventually turned up the car. We were on our way three hours after we had stopped for an ice cream cone that wound up costing us more than $70.

I still don't like ice cream cones!

PAT'S CAR

I hate to admit it, but my friend Pat was a scofflaw, a terrible-sounding name for a person who doesn't pay his parking fines.

Pat and I were graduate students together in the early 1950s. He was a bright young man and a talented writer, but in practical matters like cars and girls, he never quite seemed to have his act together. Socially he gave the appearance of one who had fallen out of a boat and had been hit on the head with an oar when he surfaced.

Despite this, we double dated. (I had a car and he didn't; I was interested in this blonde who served coffee at the drugstore, and she had a friend; you know the routine.) When he sought to purchase a used car, I advised him about what to look for and told him I had had good luck with the V8s of the thirties. I didn't see the '35 Ford coupe he purchased for $125 before he drove it home, but I did help him replace the rear spring when it broke. I also helped him seal the leaky radiator with "water glass," and I jump started it for him when the battery was dead, until the Iowa winter made it impractical to try to keep it running.

At Christmas break, I prepared to drive home to South Dakota for the holidays while Pat prepared to spend the vacation with his family in Atlanta. The old Ford wouldn't start, so Pat left it parked in front of his rooming house and took the bus.

When I returned three or four days later, the Ford was gone. I learned from the landlord that the police had towed it away.

Since Pat did not plan to return until the end of the vacation period (at least another ten days), I envisioned storage charges increasing day by day and decided I should rescue the old Ford before the amount against it increased another 50 or 60 dollars.

I went to the police station, expecting to have to convince the authorities that I was acting in Pat's behalf by trying to redeem the car as quickly and as cheaply as possible. To my surprise, I got good-natured cooperation, but no car. Mysteriously, no one in the police station could find any trace of it. When I pointed it out to them in the police lot, they shuffled through the files again and told me they couldn't find any paperwork on the car. It would be impossible, they said, to do anything about it without proper records.

When Pat returned to the campus two weeks later, I offered to drive him to the police station to redeem his car. He offered an excuse, which suggested to me that he might not have the money to get it out of hock. I offered to lend him what it would take, and again he demurred.

I let the matter ride. So did Pat, for a week, two weeks, a whole month. In fact, he never did go after the car. Later, I learned from his roommate that when the police towed the car in, they found the glove box stuffed with parking tickets totalling more than $300 on the $125 car.

I married the blonde the next year, and nearly 40 years later she still tolerates my fooling with old Fords.

SUMMONS

In February of 1955, I had completed a temporary assignment in Washington, D.C., and was preparing to return to my home in Iowa. During our days in the nation's capital, Rita had been working in Brentanto's, a prestigious bookstore in the downtown area.

In preparation for our move, she had saved several strong cartons for packing. On the evening of her last day, I drove into the alley at the rear of the bookstore to load the boxes into the trunk. When I emerged from the store with an armload of boxes, I found a policeman writing a ticket.

I remonstrated to no avail. It was illegal to park in the alley, and having already started writing the ticket, there was no way he could void it. (I have since learned from a retired D.C. policeman that this was true.) I ignored the ticket and left for Iowa the following morning.

Nearly two years later I received at my Iowa address a registered letter stating that I owed the District of Columbia three dollars in unpaid traffic fines, and unless I paid the amount due with dispatch, the Sheriff of Johnson County, Iowa, would receive a warrant requesting him to apprehend me to obtain payment of the fine. Further, the letter stated, I would be liable for any process and service costs incurred, should such action be necessary.

I don't really think they would have gone to those lengths for a $3.00 parking ticket, but envisioning court costs and bailiff's fees mounting rapidly, I wasn't about to find out. I sent the District of Columbia officials three dollars.

A MATTER OF TIME

Parking tickets have always been vexatious, but the most vexing one I ever received was written in the little town of Ravenna, Ohio.

I was on an errand in that city and knew I was running close to the end of my meter time. Checking my watch carefully, I hurried back to my car a couple of minutes before time on the meter was to expire.

To my dismay, I found a ticket under my windshield wiper. To make matters worse, the meter still had four minutes to run. Information on the ticket read that it had been written at 11:00 a.m. I checked my watch. It read 10:56.

I briefly considered chasing the fat meter maid who was waddling down the next block, but decided instead to take the case to City Hall, a couple of blocks in the other direction.

When I arrived at the window that had been handily set up for the payment of parking fines, I handed the woman on duty the ticket and asked her if she would please check the clock on the wall behind her. She gave me a puzzled look and turned.

''What time is it?'' I asked.

''It's two minutes to eleven,'' she said.

''Good!'' I responded. ''This ticket isn't written yet!'' I pointed to the time it had purportedly been written, then tore the document in half, folded it and tore it again, and handed her the pieces.

Ignoring her protests, I returned to my car.

BY THE NUMBERS

COMPUTERS

Not long after automobiles began to run on city streets, officials came up with various schemes to register, number, or license them, both for revenue purposes and to keep track of the highly mobile newfangled contraptions. Early systems assigned numbers to individual cars and required owners to display those numbers on the vehicle in a highly visible manner—on front or rear, or both. In many states, the numbers served not only to identify a specific car, but also to indicate the county or city in which the vehicle was owned.

By the numbers — The Ohio Motor Vehicle Department's computer correctly identified the license number on this 1966 Mustang for the Boy Scout troop.

Computer error — The Ohio Motor Vehicle Department's new computer recorded it had no record of the license number on this 1967 Ford Country Squire.

Eventually, highly complex systems of vehicle identification numbers and certificates of title keyed to the license number became the rule in all states. It was only a matter of time before the identification numbers and record of ownership would be entered in computer files that could be searched quickly for information about stolen vehicles or autos involved in hit-and-run accidents. Ohio developed such a system in the mid-1960s.

At that time, I was leader of a troop of Webelo Scouts (eight- to ten-year-olds) who aspired to become Boy Scouts. For our monthly activity in November, we visited the local Highway Patrol headquarters. The patrolmen, proud of their newly-installed computer system which would identify make, model, name, and address of the owner of any automobile registered in the state from the license number, were eager to demonstrate it for the boys.

We gave the patrolman on duty the license number of the Ford station wagon I was driving to bring the boys to the patrol headquarters. To the embarrassment of the patrolman, the machine reported "No record of this vehicle." I was somewhat concerned also, because to the youngsters in my troop, the report suggested that there might be something not quite appropriate about my ownership of the car.

As a further test of the system, we gave the operator the license number of my Mustang, which was in numerical sequence with that of the wagon, since I had purchased the tags at the same time. The computer quickly responded, "Yellow 1966 Mustang coupe, owner, Murvin H. Perry, 511 Harvey Street, Kent, Ohio."

The boys were suitably impressed, and the miss on the previous entry was soon forgotten. I dismissed it from my thoughts also until about a month later. At about 4:00 a.m., I was awakened by my front doorbell. I arose and peered sleepily from my bedroom window. There was a police cruiser in the driveway. I hastened to the front door.

The officer asked perfunctorily if I was Mr. Perry, and came directly to the point: "Do you own a 1967 Ford station wagon?"

"Yes," I said, wondering what problem with the car could bring the police at this hour of the morning.

"Where is it?" he demanded.

"In the garage," I replied.

"Are you sure?" he continued.

"It was when I went to bed."

"What time was that?"

"Between ten and eleven o'clock."

"Is the license plate still on it?"

I couldn't respond with certainty since I really hadn't looked, but I said, "I think so. It was the last time I noticed."

The policeman insisted on looking in the garage, so I opened the garage door and let him in. When he had satisfied himself that the car in question was indeed in the garage, and that the license plate was properly attached to the bumper, he explained.

"We got a call from the Indiana Highway Patrol. They found a note in the women's rest room at a plaza on the Indiana Turnpike. The note read, 'Help! I'm being kidnapped!' and listed this license number, which the computer traced to you."

On a crumpled piece of paper, he had written the license number of my station wagon—the car the computer had been unable to find only a brief time before.

''Naturally we had to check it out,'' he apologized, lamely. ''Sorry to get you up at this hour of the morning.''

In retrospect, it is fairly easy to surmise what happened. At the time, I was associate dean of the college, with responsibilities for enforcing academic standards. In those days of student dissent and unrest, I was obviously not the most popular dean on campus. I suspect some imaginative student had conceived the scheme and dropped off the note on the way home for the Christmas holiday as a means of getting even for whatever penalty I had imposed.

WRONG NUMBER

In another instance (which was probably more the result of human error than computer fault), I received a phone call at my desk one fall afternoon.

''Are you Mr. Perry?'' an angry voice demanded.

''Yes,'' I replied, ''What can I do for you?''

''Do you own a 1976 Caprice?'' the voice asked.

I don't hear well, and I thought he said Capri, so I said, ''I do, but it's not a '76.''

At the time, I owned two, which my boys drove to school, one a '73 and one a '74. I expected there had been an accident. I hoped it was not serious, but I was not prepared for what came next.

''Are you going to come down here and pay for that gas, or do I have to send the sheriff after you?'' the voice demanded.

I was certain neither of my boys would intentionally leave a filling station without paying for gasoline, and if they had, I would certainly want to make it right. I tried to sort it out:

''Was it the dark brown car or the cream colored one?''

''Brown, hell; it was green! I took down the license number and checked it with the police. It's your '76 Chevy, and by God, you better pay for the gas or I'll have the law on you.''

I did also own a '76 Chevy, but it was a pickup truck.

''What was the license number you checked?'' I asked.

He recited a number, which I recognized as the plate number of my pickup.

''But that number's on a blue pickup truck!'' I told him.

''The hell it is!''

''You were talking about a green car. When did this happen?''

"That's right," he said, "a green '76 sedan. You drove off without paying about half an hour ago.

I was certain now the man had made a mistake.

"Look, mister, you must have made a mistake with the number. I'm driving that truck myself, and it's been parked outside my office all afternoon. If you'll tell me where your station is, I'll bring it down and clear this up."

With some resentment, I drove to his establishment. He looked at me and the truck and checked the number of the license plate. He admitted I was not the person who had left without paying for the gas.

He started to mutter something about changing the plate. I said:

"Mister, that license plate has been on that truck for at least two years, and you've carried this accusation about far enough. You must have got at least one of the numbers wrong when you looked at the license plate."

I could see he didn't want to admit he was wrong, but he was resigned that he couldn't pin the unpaid bill on me.

I drove back to the office feeling I could have been a lot nastier about his mistake; but what the hell—he was out a $17 tankful of gas.

CHAUFFEUR'S LICENSE

To accompany the anecdotes about computer errors, I must offer one about a foul-up that was not the computer's fault.

Recently, during a visit with retired friends in Florida, we remarked about an impressive stretch limousine with a "for sale" sign on it parked on a residential lawn. Our host impishly inquired of his wife, "Should we buy you a car?"

Her straight-faced reply was, "I could get a uniform and hire out as a limousine service, since I already have a chauffeur's license."

Knowing that Jean, a sprightly grandmother, had once worked for a spy outfit that was so secret it operated out of the Library of Congress, I sensed an interesting cloak and dagger tale might be about to unfold.

"You have a chauffeur's license?" I repeated. "What did you do that required that?"

As her husband chuckled, she explained:

"When we moved to Florida, we decided we would get Florida driver's licenses, so I got the booklet and studied up on all the local laws and regulations.

"When we went to take the examination, I didn't notice that Ray's was different from mine, but he whipped through his in a few minutes, while I was struggling with questions such as, 'How far from the stalled vehicle do you place the flares?' and 'How long should the tow line be?' Things I couldn't remember ever seeing in the booklet.

"When I finally finished it, I took it to the girl at the counter, who scored it and came back with the papers to issue the license. As she began to complete the forms, she gave me a quizzical look and said, 'You want a chauffeur's license?'

" 'No,' I replied. 'I just want an ordinary driver's license.'

" 'Oh dear,' she said, as she turned to her fellow clerk. 'They gave this lady the wrong examination. They gave her the test for a chauffeur's license. What do I do now?'

" 'Well, how did she do?' the other clerk inquired.

" 'She passed,' the first clerk replied.

" 'Well then, issue her a chauffeur's license,' the second clerk advised.

"And so," Jean concluded, "even though I've never driven a bus or an eighteen wheeler, and might have trouble with a pickup truck, I'm licensed to drive them by the State of Florida!"

THE DOUBLE NICKEL

Although I often chaffed under the 55 mph speed limit, I had four good reasons to appreciate it. They were named Mark, Scott, Todd, and Chris! The limit was imposed in the early '70s, just as our four sons were coming to the learning-to-drive age. Remembering some of my own boyhood escapades with open country roads and cars with speeds that topped out at 65 to 70 (a good Ford V8 would hit 85), I was apprehensive about the responsibility of teaching four young fellows to drive high-powered cars in metropolitan traffic.

I anticipated there would be accidents, but—with reduced speeds—I was relieved that prospects for disastrous results were also reduced. At the same time, the local police would be enforcing a speed limit that I would have felt obligated to impose but would probably have been powerless to enforce.

There were speeding tickets. Todd came in one evening after having taken the old stick-shift Capri out on the new four-lane at the south edge of town and surrendered his license along with his ticket. (I didn't know the old heap would go that fast.) All the young fellows used the stretch to try out their wheels. The police knew it and kept regular watch there.

Mark had a lane-changing brush and reported it directly to our insurance company. His pride suffered greater damage than the Mustang, but our insurance agent later called me to say that Mark had conducted himself admirably and that he hoped his two sons of similar age would behave in as creditable mannner.

Scott tagged a fender on a beat-up rice burner when he was pulling away from a filling station, leaving scars on the Capri and his wallet. Chris was sideswiped by a redneck in a pickup truck making a left turn before Chris cleared the intersection. And Todd overshot a corner on a country road late one night. He had to be rescued when the mud, trapped in the front wheel that had gone off the road, built up such an imbalance that he was afraid to drive the car home.

Most were small mishaps, but there were two that could have been serious. One involved some of Scott's friends who snatched his keys one night when we were away and ''borrowed'' Rita's Capri for a midnight joyride. The ride ended in a cul-de-sac where they took out a mailbox and collapsed a front wheel when they crashed into the curb. Loyal to his friends, Scott helped them replace the wheel with the spare and nurse the car home.

The following morning they purchased a new wheel, but there were other signs of the incident they could not hide. When Mark started to drive to school, he found the car did not steer well. Because of a bent stabilizer bar, the left front wheel rubbed on the fender when he attempted to turn. It took the three would-be drivers several months to pay for the repairs in installments from their grocery bagging wages.

Scott was responsible for the incident that came closest to being disastrous. On a side street in Kent, a series of dips produced a genuine thrill ride when negotiated at high speed. One summer, when I was away for a day, Scott took his brothers for a ride over the ''bumps.'' In his youthful enthusiasm, he misjudged the speed. The Olds Custom Cruiser became airborne at a nose-dive angle. When the car came down, the front crossmember of the frame plowed a two-foot furrow in the asphalt. A strut that braced the bumper tore off and punctured the pan of the automatic transmission.

By the time I returned, the boys had carefully pushed the disabled station wagon home with their mother's Capri, creating only a few nicks and dings on the bumper of her car. They had removed the punctured oil pan to have it welded. I helped them complete the repair, thankful that no one had been hurt and that they had not compounded the damage by trying to drive the car after the transmission fluid had been lost.

BOY SCOUTS

Since this chapter began with a Boy Scout story, let me add one more scout story here. In the early days of Sports Car Club of America racing at Nelson's Ledges in Ohio, our scoutmaster was a member of the SCCA. Through his association with the club, he arranged for our troop to camp at the track during race week and to help club members with gate duty and gofer chores. The troop was divided into crews, which alternated camp responsibilities and track assignments.

One misty morning with a slight drizzle falling, the squad assigned to mess cook duty seemed to be having trouble getting everything in order for breakfast. By the time they were ready to serve, the rest of the troop members were restlessly waiting in line with their eating utensils.

My second son, Scott, was first in line. As he approached the steaming pan from which his fellow scout was serving, he eagerly thrust out his plate. The mess cook served a huge spoonful of something that hit the plate with a splat. Scott looked at it curiously and asked with a note of hope in his voice:

"What is it? Scrambled eggs?"

"No," the server replied. "It's pancakes."

The concessionaire did a lot of business with the boys from the scout troop that day.

Is it pancakes? — Boy Scouts line up for breakfast during camp out at Sports Car Club of America rally at Nelson's Ledges in Ohio.

IT'S A SMALL WORLD

TRAVEL CHANGES EVERYTHING

I have a collection of "small world" stories assembled over the years. A couple of them relate to automobiles.

The first occurred in the early days of World War II. Just prior to enlisting in the Seabees, I had traveled to California to see a girlfriend whose family had left their South Dakota farm for jobs in the aircraft industry in California. One evening, we were driving from Whittier back to Rivera when a car that had been following us came alongside and signaled for us to pull over.

The driver apologized for stopping us and said, "I noticed your Brookings County license plates and wondered if you know the Haroldsons?"

"You mean Gil Haroldson of Bruce?"

"Yes. We are cousins. We've been out here 28 years, but we always like to meet people from South Dakota."

As a matter of fact I did know the Haroldsons. My father had rented a farm from Gil, and it was on that farm that I had gone to the field with four horses and a gang plow when I was 11 years old. In addition, Gil's son Donald and I had been friends in high school. I had once wrecked his car when I was paying more attention to the girl I was courting than to my driving and smacked into the back of a truck at a stop light.

Later, when I was detached from my Seabee unit in New Caledonia, I wandered through the vast receiving station at Noumea. There was a party going on somewhere in the several acres of tents. I made my way toward the music and discovered that the sailor playing the banjo was the son of my mother's girlhood best friend. Our mothers had maintained contact for some years after they had grown and married. I could remember playing with him when we were both in short pants, but I had not seen him since we were about four years old. Since I knew most of the country ballads of those days, I joined in the party, and we had a great reunion until the wee hours of the morning. The following day, I shipped out for Guam and I've not seen him since.

Years later, as I lounged around a motel swimming pool in Los Angeles, a young woman asked if I would use her camera to make a picture of her and her husband, since they were on their honeymoon. I accepted the assignment and introduced myself.

"Oh," said the young woman excitedly, "You're a journalism teacher. I'll bet you know my uncle."

She mentioned the name of the recent administrator of the journalism school at my alma mater. In this instance, I did know him, but not well.

When Rita and I visited Russia, I was checking our coats in the Variety Theater in Leningrad when I heard someone speaking English behind me. A short, white-haired man was talking to Rita.

"What part of the States are you from?" he asked.

Rita told him we were from Kent State, near Cleveland.

"Oh, Kent State," the man said. "Do you know Art Wheeler there?"

"Of course I know Art," I replied. "He's head of the philosophy department."

"Well," the man said, "My name is Ed Falkowski, and I'm originally from Toledo. I came over here in the '30s to work in the mines. Art was a kid growing up in the neighborhood when I left."

I made note of the man's name and called Art when I returned to the campus. Art chuckled and said:

"Yeah, he worked in the mines all right. The SOB was a writer for *The Daily Worker*!"

Some years later, on the eve of an appearance on the program of a major organization concerned with international education, I was dining with one of the other speakers. The head of the organization, who happened to come from Kansas State, where I had formerly taught, came into the dining room. My dinner companion recognized him and said, "I want to meet him. His old boss and I used to be roommates."

The name of the president of the university the man was from flashed through my mind, and I said, "His old boss? Do you mean Jim McCain?"

"Yes," he said. "Do you know Jim? He and I roomed together in prep school in North Carolina! Small world, isn't it?"

With this, I launched into my story about the man in the Leningrad theater. When I got to the point where the man stuck out his hand and said, "I'm Ed Falkowski," my dinner companion put down his fork and said, "Ed Falkowski. I knew him in Moscow in 1934."

Not long ago, I was attending a national professional meeting in Oklahoma and dining with a fellow professional whom I had known since we were graduate assistants together nearly 30 years ago. We were discussing my impending retirement and my old-car hobby. Vern said he had a brother-in-law who was interested in old cars. I had earlier arranged to look at a car in a little town in southern Kentucky during the following week and remembered that he had roots somewhere in that part of Kentucky. I dug the address of the car owner from my wallet and said to Vern, "Maybe you can tell me where this is."

He looked at the address and laughed.

"I sure can," he said. "That's my brother-in law!"

(The car was a rusty junker. I didn't buy it.)

This whole business of small world was brought to mind again recently when I was at a party for newcomers in our community. When one of the newcomers introduced himself as being from Newark, Ohio, I inquired if he knew Frank Spencer, who had edited the local newspaper there. He said he and Frank had attended high school together. Frank and I went to Russia together when the Iron Curtain was first lifted. Small world. Isn't it?

FAR FROM HOME

Probably the most fateful small world instance I experienced involved my enlistment in the Seabees during World War II.

Risking the wrath of the draft board, I had stretched a deferment to harvest the fall crops in South Dakota into a short visit with a young woman I was courting in Los Angeles. When the notice for me to report for induction arrived at the farm, I was nearly 2000 miles away. Since the distance was too far to travel in time to meet the induction order, I determined I would enlist in California to avoid the local draft. That way I would also have my choice of services.

I went first to the recruiting offices of the U.S. Marines. I failed the vision test. Since I was determined to avoid the infantry, my next call was at the Navy recruiting station.

The Navy physical was less demanding and I was accepted, but I was told that the Navy had a quota limit on the number of enlistments it could accept and I would have to wait approximately six weeks before I could be sworn in.

This would not help. The reporting deadline back home was now only three days away. Not even the fastest train could get me back in time. As I turned to leave the room, which was filled with more than 100 recruiters working at desks, I heard a voice from clear in the back of the room call out, "Hey, Perry, what are you doing here?"

The voice belonged to Harley Andresen, who had attended South Dakota State College with me during the previous summer.

I explained my problem.

"That will be easy to fix," he said. "I can enlist you in the Seabees."

"What are the Seabees?" I inquired.

He explained they were a construction branch of the Navy comparable to the Army Engineer Corps. My enthusiasm was immediately kindled.

"Sign me up!" I said.

Within the hour I took the oath that started me on an eventful service adventure that took me across a succession of idyllic South Pacific Islands.

Later, as I was passing time during a layover in Hawaii on my first trip home in four years, I learned that my brother-in-law, who was several years younger than I, had enlisted in the Navy and was stationed at Kanehoe Bay. I arranged to visit him. Although he had been in the service less than six months, he yelled, "It's good to see somebody from home!" as he raced across the parking lot to meet me when I alighted from the bus.

FIXIN' CARS

UNCLE ED'S BROKEN "EX"

My first recollection of car trouble is a shadowy one. It involved my Uncle Ed and his 490 Chevrolet. From what I understood of conversation I could hear, I learned he had broken an "ex." He, my father, and Grandpa Eichel had hitched a team of horses to the car and were towing it home by lantern light. I wasn't very old, but I remember my mother was driving our Model T and my little brother Lyle was asleep on the backseat.

Progress was slow. For a reason I didn't understand, Grandpa and Uncle Ed had tied a board along the running board on the left side of the car. It didn't quite reach the front wheel. It was secured to the bumper at the rear, and a second rope held it suspended from the door handle. A third had been tied at the front, but it had a lot of slack in it from where it was tied on the hood, and it kept pulling out of place.

Uncle Ed managed the horses, Grandpa carried the lantern, and Dad walked alongside the car, pushing the board back into place when it swung away from the car. Mother explained that it was to keep the "ex" from coming out and the wheel from falling off.

They towed it into the farmyard and unhitched the horses in front of the lean-to on the barn where the car was kept. Then they pushed it backward into the shed.

I thought this too was silly, because at least when the car was broken one should take it to the garage. But the adults agreed it would be better to fix it themselves. They thought the guy who ran the local garage was an idiot. He had tightened the middle main bearing on Dad's Model T and caused the crankshaft to break.

There was some discussion of how they might get the broken stub of the "ex" out. They suggested using a snare and a piece of wire so they wouldn't have to take the whole rear end apart.

At that point, I must have fallen asleep. I don't know whether the snare worked or not. It was some time before I saw Uncle Ed again.

By then the Chevy had been repaired. It must have been a good repair, because it lasted until Uncle Ed bought a new Pontiac in 1929.

It was much later that I learned that ''ex'' was apparently a local vernacular for axle. People in the California shops and the Seabee unit I served in during World War II didn't know what I was talking about. Though it was used regularly in talking about the part that attached wheels to cars, wagons, and farm machinery when I was young, I haven't heard the term in years—not even in the area where I grew up.

SMOKE

''I've just done a terribly stupid thing,'' my friend said on the phone. ''I need your advice.'' There was genuine concern in his voice. He explained:

''I was servicing my daughter's car. I topped off the power steering reservoir, and I was going to put a bottle of fuel injector cleaner in the gas tank when I was interrupted by the telephone. I set the bottles down in the driveway.

''When I returned from the phone call, I picked up one of the bottles and poured it into the gas tank. As I was preparing to throw the empty bottle in the trash, I realized I had poured the power steering fluid into the gas tank. What should I do?''

I tried to think quickly. What's in power steering fluid? Castor oil, glycerine, silicone. ''How big was the bottle?'' I asked.

''It was the same size and shape as the cleaner,'' he said. ''About 12 ounces. Should I drain the tank?''

Twelve ounces in 15 to 20 gallons of gasoline. I pondered.

''I don't think it will hurt anything,'' I reassured him. ''I'd top off the tank, put the cleaner in, and drive it out.''

''You mean we can clean the injectors at the same time we gum them up?''

''I don't think it will bother the injectors,'' I said. ''The engine may smoke a little, but I don't think you'll even notice it.''

I forgot the incident. A few days later we were lounging on his patio and he made reference to the incident, saying his daughter had said there was quite a bit of smoke.

His wife added that a fellow motorist had stopped the daughter to tell her the car was on fire.

I scoffed. ''Certainly you are exaggerating. There wouldn't be that much smoke.''

''Yes there is,'' the wife insisted. ''It was bad.''

At this point we all climbed into the hot tub and the daughter departed on an errand.

She returned shortly in a panic, ''Daddy, Daddy, I think my car's on fire!''

I first thought she had gotten into the spirit of the joke and was continuing to rag her father about his mistake. But I soon realized the girl was serious, so I grabbed a towel and raced to the driveway.

The car was enveloped in steam. I could see immediately there was no fire, just a cloud of steam boiling from under the hood.

My friend fumbled for the release lever and lifted the hood. Steam was hissing from a radiator hose directly over the exhaust manifold. When things cooled sufficiently to enable me to see in the engine compartment, I found that the front of the manifold was covered with a white residue from the evaporated coolant.

What the daughter had identified as smoke for a week had been a pinhole leak in the radiator hose that squirted on the manifold and turned to steam. Now with the coolant nearly all gone, the car had overheated.

Contemplating the prospect of a ruined engine, my friend was clearly exasperated with the daughter, who protested, ''But Daddy, you said it would smoke!''

Fortunately it was a short errand and the overheating had caused no serious damage.

SHATTERED FAITH

I have a profound distrust of automobile mechanics. It's more than a skepticism created by media stories of innocent female reporters being charged hundreds of dollars to repair an engine miss caused by a shorted spark plug. It is based on a lifetime of experience with misdiagnosed, misrepresented, and improperly performed repairs, all of which were billed for at hourly rates far above my earnings as an educator.

The earliest I recall involved my father's 1919 Model T which had developed an unhealthy ''thump.'' Dad took it to the local garage, where the mechanic diagnosed a ''loose main bearing'' and removed the oil pan to repair it. Those of you who remember the early T Models recall that until about 1923, they were equipped with a ''short'' oil pan, which meant that both end main bearings could be reached only by taking the engine out of the car and removing the crankcase.

Dad's mechanic may have meant well, but since he couldn't reach the two end bearings, he settled for removing shims from the center bearing, which seemed to satisfactorily quiet the car. At least it was satisfactory until the crankshaft broke shortly thereafter, because running with the two end bearings loose allowed it to flex until metal fatigue caused it to break.

Later I watched an unknowledgeable mechanic unsuccessfully substitute part after part on a customer's balky vehicle until he could get the inoperative starting system to function. That may well have been the appropriate "trial and error method" of diagnosing the problem. But when a part failed to correct the ailment, he did not remove it; he simply left it in place and billed for it at the full retail rate.

That may have been the regimen for the service station mechanics and the small "private garages," but Mr. Goodwrench's promoters will claim the service departments of large dealerships have long been staffed with skilled mechanics who have attended schools to be trained to repair the specific cars the dealership sells. They are, we are told, equipped with specialized instruments to diagnose any problem speedily and efficiently.

In 1950, I owned one of the first Oldsmobiles with automatic transmission. My father delighted in showing his unbelieving farm friends that "Murvin's new car doesn't have a clutch."

At something over 70,000 miles, however, the rear pump failed to function, one of the bands burned out, and the transmission refused to shift. I took it to the Oldsmobile dealership, where an obliging mechanic quickly disassembled it and showed me the failed parts. He indicated it would be necessary to order replacement parts, adding that it would take several days to get them.

The delay stretched into a week, then two, and was dragging on to nearly a month when I went into the shop to see what the holdup was. I found the transmission still in pieces in a box on the workbench, with no evidence of new parts or efforts to reassemble it. The mechanic who had taken it apart was not present. I inquired of other workers who finally admitted: "He won't be back until next week. He's in Minneapolis attending transmission school."

He later returned to fix the transmission satisfactorily, but I think I paid for his schooling.

EXTENDED WARRANTY

Although I have had a few happy experiences, my appraisal of auto mechanics has not changed much over the years. Whenever I find it necessary to have repairs made, I apprehensively clutch my wallet tightly as I approach their service bays.

Not long ago, the transmission on Rita's Buick Century required replacement. Although we had paid a premium for a five-year, 50,000 mile extended warranty, the trouble occurred five years and one month after we had purchased the car, with the odometer reading 51,327.

I will credit General Motors for agreeing to split the $1,300 cost of replacing the transmission, although I calculate that $650 was approximately the real cost of the rebuilt unit they were supplying. The fact that a second replacement was required before the vehicle operated satisfactorily, and there were attendant troubles associated with the replacement, is not to their credit.

The trouble occurred at a most inopportune time. We were preparing for a cross-country trip that required us to be in Iowa by the weekend. Because Rita had reported that the automatic transmission had been making some foolish shifts, when we were having the car serviced in preparation for the trip, we asked the garage to check the transmission. Their mechanic's mournful diagnosis was that a clutch was failing and that the transmission would have to be replaced. "The problem is characteristic of that model, and GM recommends replacing the transmission with an improved unit rather than repairing the ailing one."

The problem was compounded by the fact that it would take at least four days to get the new unit from Atlanta and another day to install it. With luck, the car would be ready by Thursday. There was a delay, however, and by Friday morning (rather than delay our departure) we reluctantly borrowed our daughter's Japanese-made sport coupe, which had a five-speed manual transmission. Although Rita had not driven a stick shift vehicle since she had learned to drive with her father's '35 Dodge, we set out for Iowa.

We left the Buick with the dealer to be repaired while we were gone and picked it up when we returned a week later. Rita complained, however, that the car had not shifted properly on the trip home from the shop, and during the following two weeks I took it back at least three times before the service manager decided the replacement transmission could not be properly adjusted and suggested we try another.

SLOPPY WORK

Installing a second replacement transmission in Rita's Buick would require another week. The first had failed on the trip home from the shop, and facing another travel deadline which dictated that we leave on the following Saturday morning, I was less than happy when I left the car on Monday.

I picked it up on Friday and it seemed to be okay. We packed and departed early Saturday morning. In a quiet block near the edge of town, I detected a scraping sound and asked Rita if the noise was coming from the radio. She couldn't pick up the sound and moved to set the cruise control as we left the city limits. To her surprise, the needle was not visible on the speedometer scale. A close look revealed it was resting at zero. The scraping noise had stopped. The odometer indicated the car had traveled seven miles since it left the dealer's shop.

We pulled into the Buick dealer's lot. Since it was Saturday morning, only a salesman was available. He suggested we could get some attention at the Buick establishment in Bristol, 25 miles away. Since it was on our route, we drove there. Their service department was also closed, but the salesman was certain the dealership at Marion, another 30 miles down the road, remained open on Saturday. We drove there, only to find it was also closed.

My first assumption was that the mechanic had improperly attached (or had failed to attach) the speedometer cable or an electrical connection that controlled the instrument. So I enlisted the aid of fellow members of my Early Ford V8 Club to examine the unknown territory of the front-wheel-drive vehicle. We could find nothing that appeared to be improperly attached.

We drove back to the local dealership, where two would-be mechanics were engaged in work on their own cars in the closed service bay. We triggered the computer's diagnostic function and deciphered the code to mean "faulty speed sensor." The younger of the mechanics described it as "a banana-shaped, electronic thing located under the dash, costing about $125 to replace." Fortunately the parts department was also closed, or I would probably have been stuck with the bill for that; but as we were considering alternatives, the other mechanic unscrewed the speedometer cable from the transmission. (I had been unable to find it until we lifted the car on a hoist.) He withdrew a two-inch stub of the cable, which had broken where the cable housing had been kinked between the transmission and the firewall. We had now located the problem, but the parts department was still closed, and we could not get a replacement cable until Monday. Since we were reluctant to undertake a thousand-mile trip on interstate highways without a speedometer, we delayed our departure for the weekend.

Monday at 7:30, I took the car in. It seemed that a cable was not readily available but would have to be acquired from a remote depot. It would be noon before I could expect the car to be ready. At noon I was still waiting as an overweight mechanic leisurely replaced the lower half of the cable housing and inserted a new cable. He slammed down the hood, gave it an indolent wipe with an orange shop rag, and brought the paperwork to the write-up girl, who had assumed the role of service manager.

She presented me a bill for $75 for parts and labor. I gave it back to her saying, "I'm not going to pay this. Your mechanic kinked that cable housing when he installed the transmission, which caused the cable to break." After an argument during which I refused to yield, she went to talk to the mechanic, who wiped his hands and came over to tell me, "It was not our fault. I installed that transmission myself, and I don't do sloppy work!"

I said again, "I won't pay it."

The girl said, "I'll have to call the service manager."

"You call him, and tell him I refuse to pay for this," I responded and drove away.

After a week in Ohio, I lifted the hood to check water and oil in preparation for the trip home. On the engine block next to the alternator, I found one of the wiping rags left by the mechanic who didn't "do sloppy work."

BRAKE PROBLEM

Before departing for a winter vacation in Florida, I took Rita's Buick to the shop for brake work. I complained that the rotors on the car seemed to be less than satisfactory since they appeared to warp in less than 25,000 miles of relatively undemanding driving.

The service manager told me it was because I had failed to have the calipers rebuilt when I had the rotors turned and that a dragging pad caused heat to build up and warp the rotors. It sounded plausible, so I paid for the complete job: new pads, rotors turned, and calipers rebuilt.

As we neared our destination in Florida, I noted that the brake pedal suddenly became spongy and the brake light on the dash came on momentarily. As soon as we were unloaded at our vacation headquarters, I checked the master cylinder and found that the rear chamber was almost empty of fluid. I nursed the car gingerly to the nearest outlet of the chain that had serviced the brakes before we left home.

Their diagnosis was that we needed a new master cylinder. I was not in a position to question that, but I did dispute the price, which came to nearly $200. The service manager patiently explained that my car took a special master cylinder that included a built-in proportioning valve to distribute the hydraulic pressure to front and back wheels while keeping both systems separate so that a leak in one would not cause total loss of braking function. I paid the bill.

Less than a week later, I noticed my son pump the brake pedal tentatively as we prepared to pull onto the notorious US 19 south of Tampa.

''Don't those brakes feel right?'' I asked.

''No, they're kinda soft,'' he replied.

We lifted the hood. We could detect brake fluid dripping from the frame behind the left front wheel. The rear chamber of the new master cylinder was nearly empty. We eased along the berm to a service station, filled the cylinder with brake fluid, and headed for another outlet of the chain three or four miles up the highway.

The service manager there examined the new master cylinder and a trace of brake fluid that ran from the lower bolt that secured it to the power brake cylinder and promised to fix it.

We busied ourselves in a nearby mall for the couple of hours he estimated it would take to fix it.

When we returned, he explained: ''We replaced the master cylinder, but we don't think that was the problem. We found that the hose to the left front caliper had not been tightened properly and was leaking at the connection.''

There was no charge for that repair.

TURN OFF THE LIGHTS

The trip through the back roads of Georgia had been pleasant, and we made better time than we had anticipated. When we stopped for an afternoon break at Lake City, Fla., we phoned ahead to friends in Tampa that they could expect us to arrive after dinner that evening. It was still light as we left the two-lane roads of the back country and headed down I-75.

As dusk began to gather, I felt a thump against the fender, as if the wheel had run over something on the road and thrown it against the car. I was puzzled because I had not seen anything on the road and my driving habit is to avoid hitting such debris if at all possible. Shortly, I felt two more similar thumps. Not long after, I heard a strange flopping sound, like the blades of a helicopter hovering overhead. I knew it was no helicopter; my right front tire was going flat. I was aware I was pushing the mileage limit on my tires. However, one had been punctured beyond repair a short time earlier, and the dealer had estimated 12,000 miles of wear remained in them and had adjusted the replacement accordingly.

I pulled as far off the road as possible and began the chore of unloading all the luggage from the trunk to gain access to the temporary spare. I had it mounted and was replacing the suitcases in the trunk when it struck me that perhaps I should turn off the headlights to conserve the battery. The thought came too late. The battery was nearly six years old. In the 15 or more minutes it had taken me to change the tire, it exhausted its charge. The car wouldn't crank.

A helpful young man stopped to offer assistance, but we could not successfully jump start with either of the two sets of jumper cables we had available. We rode with him to the next interchange, where we engaged a tow truck to rescue us. The truck operator also tried vainly to jump start the car before loading it up and hauling it seven miles to his station.

At the station, a quick charge soon boosted the battery to operating strength, but the station did not have in stock a tire to fit the car. Since it was near closing time, we abandoned hope of getting a new tire that evening and opted to settle into a motel until the next day. The closest motel, however, was seven miles back along the freeway, which we negotiated lamely on the little rubber doughnut of a temporary spare.

On the following morning, we purchased a new set of tires and forgot the matter until we were safely installed in our vacation condo with the car parked under a streetlight out front.

On Sunday morning as we readied for church, we found the battery was dead. After the earlier experience, I concluded that it had this time given up, and I borrowed a car to go for a replacement.

The next day, however, the new battery was dead. I was able, however, to get it jump started and took it back where I had bought it. They checked it, pronounced it okay, but rather than charge it up, replaced it with another new one.

I was happy until I went to start the car the next day. Again I found the battery barely able to start the car. I made certain to drive far enough that day, to insure the battery would be fully charged.

When I arose the next morning and looked out at the row of cars parked out front, I saw all were covered with dew except mine. There was a dry spot in the center of the top.

A light dawned. The dome light! Burning all night, it had created heat enough to dry an area not quite two feet in diameter. When we had arrived, we had switched on the dome light to unload, and with the car parked under the streetlight at night and in the bright sunlight during the day, we had failed to notice we had not turned it off.

SOME THOUGHTS ABOUT CARS AND LIFE

THE CAR FELL ON ME—AND IT SAVED MY LIFE

The '71 Olds Custom Cruiser station wagon was on its last legs, but we were reluctant to give it up. From a standstill, it moved grudgingly and noisily for long periods before it would shift up and get going at highway speeds. It was apparent that the torque converter was locked in the high range and was not functioning properly at low speeds. It would have to be replaced.

My son Scott and I unbolted the transmission and installed a replacement converter. To accomplish the exchange, we propped the car up on cinder blocks with short pieces of two-inch lumber laid across the web faces. That was a mistake.

As I was snugging down the last bolt in the transmission mount, Scott undertook to connect the drive shaft at the differential. To get it in place, he gave it a whack, and the car moved ever so little on its chocks. The jar was sufficient to cause one of the cinder blocks it was resting on to crumble. When it gave way, the weight shifted and the car came crashing down. I sensed that it was falling and scooted from under it as fast as I could, but I was too late. The frame rail came down on my chest, and I was trapped with one arm and one leg still under the vehicle. The car was still on its wheels, but the clearance was insufficient to accommodate my body.

Although I was quickly freed, I knew I was injured badly enough to require medical attention. My left hand, which had been across my chest when I was trapped, was scraped badly as I yanked it free. It was starting to bleed and I recognized the symptoms of shock as I slipped out of my coveralls and allowed myself to be driven to the hospital. I experienced no impairment of movement, however, until I got to the X-ray room, where I found I could not command the muscles necessary to climb onto the X-ray table or to turn over on it as the radiologist requested.

Although the paralysis persisted for about six weeks, during which time I was unable to initiate the movement necessary to rise from a chair, I was relieved when the physician read the X-ray and reported: "You're bent all to hell, but nothing is broken. You do have a severe double hernia that should be patched up."

He referred me to a surgeon who looked me over and said, "Yeah, you need to have that belly mended, but I'm not going to cut you open until I have clearance from a cardiologist!"

This should not have been a surprise to me. I knew I was having some trouble. I expected it. Only one member of my mother's family had lived to be 60. Heart disease had claimed them all. I was already past the age that most of them had attained.

For the previous ten years I had suffered from shortness of breath and a sharp pain near the base of my throat when I first engaged in strenuous exercise, but it would abate after a minute or two of effort, and I would be able to function as if I had "gotten a second wind." I had persisted in playing volleyball and tennis two or three times a week, and I regularly walked or rode a bicycle to work as the best method I knew to ward off what I considered to be inevitable.

Now I was being made to face it. Getting to see a cardiologist would present a problem. We were relatively new in the community, and just getting to see any kind of doctor usually meant a long period of waiting for an appointment. In a newcomer's group, Rita had become friends with the wife of a physician, who was also new to the community. He turned out to be a cardiologist and volunteered to look me over. He came to the house on Sunday afternoon and, within five minutes, determined I would need a treadmill evaluation, which he scheduled for me at the local hospital during the next week.

After a short workout, he advised: "You have some problems, but I think we can relieve them with medication." He prescribed a regimen of Inderal which indeed put me in shape to undergo surgery for the hernia repair during the Christmas holiday from school.

After the surgery, however, I seemed to recover slowly. In fact I simply could not get up and get going as I previously had. I reached the point where I could not walk uphill without stopping to rest. The doctor took another look and said, "Well, it's obvious we are not controlling this with medication. I think we must have angiograms to see what's wrong."

In the "cath-lab" I listened to the physicians clustered around the monitor clucking about whatever was going on inside me that was hidden from my view. I heard one say, "It's not a question of whether, but when." I was wheeled back to my room, and my cardiologist friend and the man who had done the catheterization came in with serious faces.

"We think surgery is indicated. We can't believe you are walking around as you are with the amount of blockage the angiograms show. Your major coronary arteries are 90 percent blocked. You have a small, natural by-pass over the back of your heart that you've obviously developed through exertion, and that's all that's keeping you alive. Most people with that much blockage would have suffered at least two heart attacks, one probably fatal. We think surgery should be undertaken immediately."

"Can it wait until school's out?" I asked. We had just begun a semester, and I was not yet a month away from the earlier surgery.

"You may not live till school's out," they replied.

"Well then," I said, "you'd better let me tell the dean I won't be in next week," and we scheduled the surgery for the following Monday morning.

It was highly successful. I was back in the office four weeks later. I've continued to play tennis, water ski, and hike mountain trails for these last ten years.

In their haste to free me, the boys punctured the oil pan of the Olds. With much labor they removed it and had it brazed. A short time after they replaced it, the timing chain slipped or broke and we gave it up. A fellow driving a Chevelle with a 427 engine responded to our "for sale" ad. He loaded it on a trailer and roared away. I assumed he was interested in the big-inch engine, but my son swears he saw the old wagon being driven around the neighboring town a year or so later.

CARS COME AND GO, BUT THE MEMORIES LINGER

From the amount of attention lavished on each, it would be easy to conclude that some men have more affection for their cars than for their women. That may be true, but for most, once a car is traded, it passes from the owner's life forever. I've traded some that I never wanted to see again, and some I speak of affectionately seem to have improved after I got rid of them. But odd circumstances have turned my attention to a couple I encountered more than once over long spans of years, almost as if the vehicles have been haunting me.

Mystery car — This 1933 Beacon was the prize in a bank night drawing at the Iowa theater in Cedar Rapids in 1933. It was driven by Miss Jessie DeLaMater for more than 30 years. It may be the only surviving example of the marque. The car was assembled by Continental Motors after the De Vaux company, that had designed and proposed to manufacture it, suffered financial difficulties and was unable to continue.

One was a 1948 Olds 98 streamliner. I purchased it at a time when I needed a car and there were only two used cars to be had in my South Dakota county seat town. One was a '47 Chevy coach that had been the prize in an American Legion lottery a couple of years before. The winner had not prized the car, and it had a tired look about it despite the dealer's efforts to polish it up for resale. The other was the Olds, a metallic green, torpedo-bodied two-door with yellow wheels and straight eight engine that appeared to be going 60 miles an hour standing still. It was a real attention getter. (It got the attention of every speed cop and highway patrolman on the road.)

It still looked new, despite the fact that it was two years old and the odometer registered more than 60,000 miles. It had been owned by a salesman for a coffin manufacturer, who called on mortuaries in the Midwest, and the highway miles had not taken a heavy toll on body or mechanical parts. The purchase price of $1,450 was within my borrowing ability, so I bought it.

I drove it while courting Rita, and reluctantly traded it for a less flashy sedan during a period of financial stress a year or so after we were married.

Sometime later, I got a phone call from a young man who wanted to know if the 96,000-plus miles then showing on the odometer was the actual mileage. I told him it was a little short because the speedometer had broken one time, and I had driven the car for more than a month before I could get it repaired. He explained that he had purchased the car but could not believe that a car with that many miles could be in such good shape. He wanted to know if I knew how to turn the odometer back so his friends would not think him foolish to buy a car with so many miles on it. I noted in the local paper sometime later that he had been involved in an accident.

More than 20 years later, I was prowling a junkyard in Iowa City looking for some hubcaps for my aging '66 Mustang when I came upon the hulk of a car that somehow caught my eye. It was lying on its top, but there was something different about the lines of its fender and body. I took another look. It was an old Olds streamliner. I peered at it closely. The wheels were gone and a coating of gray grime covered the paint, but the car looked familiar. I rubbed the grime from a protected spot. It was green. I stopped to peer inside. It was my old car! With a piece of stuffing from the rotted upholstery, I rubbed the face of the odometer and strained to read the upside-down dial. The yellowed numbers read just under 97,000 miles. The hapless young man obviously hadn't driven it very far. Not many parts had been salvaged from the hulk. Obviously there hadn't been many like it in the community for it to have served as a donor.

The other car of coincidence was a 1933 Beacon I found on the streets of Cedar Rapids one day in 1961 when I was reporting for the *Gazette*. The car was parked in front of city hall. Its owner worked there and parked the car regularly on the street, but because of its resemblance to an early model Plymouth, it had failed to attract attention.

The owner was Miss Jessie Belle DeLaMater, the city treasurer. The only car she ever owned, she had won it brand new in a bank night drawing at the local Iowa theater in 1933 (on the second drawing, after the holder of the first ticket was found not to be present). She maintained—perhaps correctly—that it might be the only one of its kind in existence.

The car was built by Continental Motors Corp. of Detroit. The company built engines for several early automobile manufacturers, even as late as the 1950s for Kaiser-Frazer, and continues to manufacture industrial engines.

Sensing material for a good feature story, I contacted Continental Motors, whose public relations officials responded that they had no information about the car-building venture in their files.

Miss DeLaMater told me that Continental built the car only one year and that it offered coaches, coupes, and sedans with three engine options. There was a modest little four-cylinder model called the Beacon, a middle-sized six-cylinder named the Flyer, and a mighty eight-cylinder powerhouse which was christened the Ace.

The Beacon's radiator medallion bore a likeness of the nation's Capitol dome and the slogan, "Powerful as the Nation." The radiator ornament was a chrome goddess similar to the silver ghost that traditionally adorns the hoods of Rolls Royce automobiles.

By 1961, Miss DeLaMater had driven the car 48,000 miles; and though it was still on its second set of tires, she had had it repainted. She had tried to enter it in an antique car show once, but the officials turned her down, telling her the car was of "special interest" but not a legitimate antique.

I have since learned that the Continental venture into car making came as a result of the collapse of the De Vaux-Hall enterprise, a project of Norman De Vaux who on two occasions attempted to operate an automobile manufacturing company.

When De Vaux ran out of money, Continental took on the job of assembling and marketing the cars. The effort was unsuccessful and was abandoned the following year.

In 1987 I read a story about a car restorer in Illinois who was restoring a 1933 Beacon he had obtained in eastern Iowa. I dug through my old files, found the Beacon feature, and sent him a copy along with an inquiry as to whether it might be the same car. The prospect that two automobiles of the limited number produced had survived seemed quite remote. It would be easy to determine if the car was the same; I had included the motor number of Miss DeLaMater's car in the feature story because, by further coincidence, it had been the same as the street number of her house.

The restorer did not respond. However, a couple of years later, I ran across his address in a file of notes for possible feature stories and called him up. By that time, he had sold the car to "someone in New England." He had not checked the serial numbers, and he no longer remembered the identity of the new owner. I remain convinced that the possibility of two surviving Beacons is somewhat remote, and I'm saving the clippings in case I run across information about the car again.

Did I say these cars haunted me?

SOME WOUNDS NEVER HEAL

The caller's voice was agitated. His words revealed why:

"Murv, did you hit my car?"

It was Jim, a young man I encountered often at his brother Gamble's store where I bought polish and supplies to maintain the 98 Olds that was my remaining link to the days before I entered graduate school. I suspected him of being interested in Rita, the pretty drugstore counter girl who was responding favorably to my courtship.

"No," I responded. "I didn't hit your car. What happened?"

"I was parked in the alley behind Linder's Tire, and someone caved in the driver's side door on my car. The guys at Linder's said you had been in to have a tire changed...."

I interrupted, "I did have Linder's fix a flat for me, but believe me, Jim, I didn't hit your car! There was someone having a lot of trouble turning around in the alley when I drove in, though. He was driving a dark brown or maroon '49 or '50 Ford. I didn't pay much attention. The car was dirty and there were some kids in the car. Maybe he did it."

"Would you know the car," he asked, "if we could find him?"

"I think he had been to Linder's too," I said. "There was something written in yellow chalk on the back tire. Where are you?"

"At the store," he said.

The store was only a short block from my rooming house. When I arrived, Jim's pea green '49 Ford was parked at the curb. The driver's side door bore the imprint of a bumper with two protruding guards. It was clear the door would require extensive repair or replacement.

The body shop said $125 minimum," Jim said. "A new door and painting could run as high as $175."

We examined the marks, which clearly did not match the spacing of the guards on the bumper of my Olds. They were, however, identical in height and spacing to those on the rear bumper of Jim's Ford.

"It was a Ford that hit it all right," I said, running my fingers over the damage. "Let's go back to Linder's."

It was near closing time, but the manager at Linder's let us go through the sales slips and work orders for the afternoon at the tire shop. We found several Fords. The time on one '49 with a left rear tire repair was logged at 2:20, just a few minutes before I had been in. We thought we had our man.

The address was out in the boondocks, several miles northeast of town. We had to ask directions a couple of times before we found the place. The evening light was beginning to fail as we drove into the farmyard.

Noting the damaged car, the obviously apprehensive farmer met us at the yard gate. A lamp had already been lighted in the house, and a yellow rectangle showed the open kitchen door. Three or four young boys whispered together in the shadows just out of the light.

"What you want here?" the farmer queried.

"Did you have a tire fixed at Linder's today?" Jim asked.

I was looking at the car parked just inside the fence.

"Yeah," he responded, "but I never hit no car!"

"I saw you turning around in the alley," I said, picking up a flashlight from the seat beside me and shining it on the rear of his car. I opened the door and moved to examine the bumper.

"You stay away from that car!" he yelled, moving too late to stop me. "You ain't got any business around here!"

I was close enough to see the bumper.

"Look here, Jim, he's still got green paint on the bumper guards!"

The excited whispers of the youngsters silenced. Jim took it from there.

"Look here, Mister," he said, "leaving the scene of an accident is a serious matter. Unless I hear from your insurance company tomorrow, I'll be sending the sheriff with a warrant for hit and run."

Deflated, the farmer agreed to report the incident to his insurance company, and Jim wrote down the name of the agent to contact on the following day. In due time the car was repaired.

Forty years later, I encountered Jim at a reunion party for Rita's high school. As we shook hands, I said, "Jim, do you remember the time you called me and asked, 'Murv, did you hit my car?'"

"Do I?" His response was immediate. "That damn Tom ________ tried to deny it when he still had paint from my car on his bumper!"

He had even remembered the farmer's name!

AFTERWORD

Over the years, my associates have often remarked, "Murv, you ought to write a book!" Sometimes the comment was prompted by genuine respect for my ideas, experience, and eloquence. Other times it was a polite way of indicating disagreement with whatever position I was expounding. I liked the idea that some considered me qualified to publish words that others might value, but I thought I expressed proper modesty with my standard response: "I would, if I had anything to say."

Actually, if I had thought anyone would take me seriously, I would certainly have been presumptuous enough to commit authorship several times. But mostly I was too busy having fun, or keeping out of trouble, to put forth the necessary effort to get it all together in a book; and there were some stories that were too painful to tell.

This manuscript wasn't meant to be a book with a message. It was written just for fun. When I began editing the newsletter for the Early Ford V8 Club in Bristol, Tenn., I supplemented news of club activities and personality sketches of club members with accounts of some of my misadventures with automobiles. I found that club members enjoyed them, and even their wives reported they were reading the newsletter. I continued to develop the accounts one incident at a time. When Dave Lewis, "Ford Country" editor for *Cars and Parts* magazine, published some Ford accounts and asked to include one in a collection he was preparing for a book, I conceived the idea that I might make a book out of the 50 to 60 "memories" I had written for the *V8 Club News*.

I was pleased that a publisher agreed to accept the manuscript and overjoyed by his editor's advice that the book should be published. I was a little taken aback when he commented that he would like to see a concluding chapter that would provide a comprehensive summary. I asked what he meant.

"Well, answers to questions like, 'Where is the American automobile industry going?' "

That was easy. Anyone can see it's been moving to Japan for the last 20 years.

"No," he said, "More like where is the American automobile industry taking us?"

I told him, "You get taken any time you believe anything a car salesman tells you and most of the time when you take your vehicle to a dealer's service area for repair."

It dawned on me that he wanted me to expound on the changes the automobile had wrought in America.

Others have documented the physical changes as cities have abandoned the trolleys and mass transportation systems that gave physical shape to their development while, at the same time, they struggled to provide new expressways and parking lots to accommodate the hordes of cars that demand room to move and to park. Today, suburban shopping malls have replaced urban department stores as centers of retailing, and commuters routinely travel farther to work than they would have traveled in a lifetime two generations ago.

Economically and socially, the automobile has come to dominate our culture. The majority of jobs in American manufacturing for years have been in automobile or automobile-related products. The average family spends more for car payments, insurance, gasoline, and repairs than for shelter or food. The most often expressed aspirations among our young people are to obtain a driver's license and to own a car.

The change has been hailed as creating a new independence and fostering individualism. The reverse may be true. We are indeed able to go where we want, when we want to go; and the automobile has provided a place of shelter for conduct we would not engage in publicly. But morals have deteriorated, and social controls over individual conduct have evaporated (not exclusively as a result of couples making out in the backseats of cars). Along with giving us individual freedom and privacy, the automobile has made most of our population slaves to monthly payments by fostering illusory values based on paint and pretense.

The mobility provided by the automobile makes it possible for an individual to hide anonymously in an impersonal urban society. At the same time, a car is the medium for many to make a personal statement. The revolutionaries of the late '60s and early '70s declared their identity by traveling in beat-up Volkswagen vans. Snobs drive underpowered, overpriced cars of obscure make to show they are concerned about the global environment, and they scorn the Detroit iron available to all. Rednecks buy four-wheel drive pickups and spend great amounts of money dressing them with every macho contrivance they can hang on them; they then fit them out with air conditioning and velour upholstery to make them more luxurious than the work truck their neighbor owns. Average guys debate the merits of Chevy, Olds, or Buick as if they didn't know they were made with common parts and the only differences are in items of trim and style. The bottom line is that the automobile has fostered a culture of excesses, some of which are mindless. The auto has not done this alone. Advertising and the mass media have contributed their share.

The good news is that the days of excesses may be over. The bad news is that the best days of the auto may have passed. As nations of the world buckle down to solve the problems of pollution of the planet and workable distribution of wealth among people, we must expect to pay more for the convenience of the automobile. In addition to purchase and operating costs, this includes frustration and delay in sharing available fuel resources as well as usable highway and parking facilities. Gone forever may be the days of the roaring muscle car, its ''King of the Road'' attitude, and the freedom to go where we want, when we want. As energy and population problems crowd in on our freedom, we will be forced to share the road.